Experiencing
Bible Science
An Activity Book for Children

By Louise Barrett Derr
Illustrated by Peggy Richards and author

WestBow Press
Bloomington, Indiana

WestBow Press books may be ordered through booksellers or by contacting:

WestBow Press
A Division of Thomas Nelson
1663 Liberty Drive
Bloomington, IN 47403
www.westbowpress.com
1 (866) 928-1240

Some of this children's edition was taken from the author's book
Experiencing Bible Science: A Lab Book for the Young at Heart

Scripture taken from the King James Version of the Bible.

Cover design: Lois Gable, Creative Touch Communications, Waxhaw, NC
Cover photo credits and identification from NASA:
Image Science and Analysis Laboratory, NASA-Johnson Space Center
22 Nov. 2004. "Earth from Space – Image Information"

Front cover photo #:
STS057-73-75
Date: June 1993
Eastern Mediterranean Sea

Back cover photo #:
STS41G-120-0056
Date: October 1984
Dead Sea Rift Valley

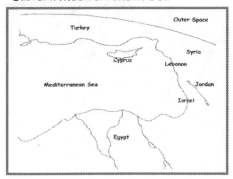

ISBN: 978-1-4908-0993-9 (sc)
ISBN: 978-1-4908-1307-3 (e)

Library of Congress Control Number: 2013917367

Printed in the United States of America.

WestBow Press rev. date: 10/9/2013

Dedicated to
my paternal grandparents
Rev. David Palmer and Olyn Reed Barrett
for their service as missionaries to Puerto Rico

Sea of Galilee

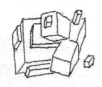

5

Table of Contents

6

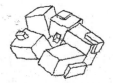

Dead Sea salt crystals

8

Acknowledgments

My first acknowledgment goes to the Holy Spirit who gave me the insight for a book about Bible science. He often woke me up at 5:00 AM and led me through the entire process of creating this book. My husband, Harry, has been supportive from the beginning in 1994. We both enjoyed discovering science as we read through the whole Bible. Our trip to Israel in March of 2007 confirmed this book appropriately represents the Holy Land.

Christian Assembly Church friends Marrie Bigelow and Elizabeth Krynsky encouraged me in the writing. The first book, *Experiencing Bible Science, an Activity Book for the Young at Heart,* took shape. It is waiting to be edited while this book for a younger audience was created.

Moving to volunteer at JAARS Inc.* has been a blessing. Everyone has been so encouraging. Peggy Pittman has critiqued from her background of growing up on the mission field. Willis Ott has checked the scripture references from his expertise helping Bible translators interpret the Word. Peggy Richards, a professional artist, volunteered her talent. Dr. Julian Pike helped with the weather and astronomy issues. Johanna Fenton, as a Wycliffe editor, reviewed the book. Julie Limmer helped with editing. Barbara Shannon made timely suggestions. Beth Brennan helped revise the index. Bob Wright helped me use Microsoft Word in a productive way. Lois Gable, a graphic artist, produced the final cover design. Children tested the activities; Annabeth Sanders, Lydia Mead, Alexis Wright, and the Meijer children, along with great comments from their parents, especially Melanie Mead and Jan Sanders.

Dr. John A. Day (Mr. Cloudman) sent the plan for the cloud types. My niece, Lauren McVey, a science teacher, reviewed the book. My sister Susan Taylor, an artist, encouraged my drawings. Children's literature professor, Dr. Janice DeLong at Liberty University in Virginia, was very encouraging. She teaches students to *create, wait,* and then *evaluate* when writing. She gave me the idea of this second book for younger children. Many more friends and family have offered books, ideas, edits, and prayers. What a blessing!

* JAARS Inc. has its headquarters in Waxhaw, North Carolina. Through partnerships worldwide, JAARS provides quality technical support services and resources to speed Bible translation for all people.

Introduction for Parents and Teachers

This book is for science discovery in the Bible, with Scripture stories and activities. Its intended audience is children at the elementary-age level. There are twenty story/-activity units, each two pages in length. There are three additional sections of Biblical science activities in nature study, crafts, and activities with adults. These supply activities for enrichment, camps, vacation Bible school and other children's groups. Step-by-step instructions are given for the activities. Measurements are in US/Imperial and Metric. Children can work on their own or in groups, with minimal adult supervision, except for the "Activities with Adults" section.

Most of the activities are safe and use readily available materials. The story activities follow along the inquiry approach style: "My Test" or "My Observation" including hypothesis (what you think will happen and when), "Items Needed", "Procedure" (how to do the activity), "Data" (record observations, details; not just watching or looking at), and "Results" (summarize data), or "Conclusions" (stating if your prediction was correct and why).

Space is given in the book for journaling (recording observations and studies) and other ideas in "My Notes." The drawings are for the enjoyment of coloring. We grant you permission to make copies of the pages if you prefer not to mark in this journal.

Basic supplies for the activities are listed below. Items could be put in a shoe box or similar container. Have the children write/label their names on personal things.

Pencil and eraser	Dictionary
Colored pencils or crayons	Scissors
Plain paper	Big, old white shirt for a lab coat
Old cotton shirt or T-shirt to cut up	Bible

Other items needed are listed with each activity. A protractor and ruler are on page 125.

Encourage each student to wear an old white shirt for a lab coat. This stimulates them to realize they are having experiences related to science. It also helps to keep their clothes clean. A patch to wear on the "lab coat" is included in the Cut-Out Page (page 125).

The student may need an introduction to the Bible. The Bible is divided into two sections: the Old Testament which includes 39 "books" of the laws, history, poetry, and prophecies of the Jews and the New Testament which includes 27 "books" of the events of the life of Jesus Christ and the activities of His disciples. Each of these 66 books has chapters with verses. Most Bibles are published with the names of the books and the chapter numbers at the top of the page so that the reader can locate the references easily. If help is needed in finding a book, most Bibles have a Table of Contents within the first few pages of the Bible. Locate the book by its page number, turn to the chapter number, and then scan down to find the desired numbered verse. As the verses are read, concentrate on the reading and how it applies to the topic. The King James Version of the Holy Bible is quoted in this text, but with the Scripture references provided, any preferred translation may be used.

"What Next?" (pages 112-113) gives a list of other things to do during and/or after completing this book. As the student matures, they may advance to the book from which this book came, *Experiencing Bible Science: An Activity Book for the Young at Heart.* It contains forty units, four pages each, and lots of related Scripture and additional activities.

Our aim is to be "skillful in all wisdom, and cunning in knowledge, and understanding science" Daniel 1:4. May we all enjoy a lifetime of learning.

"My Personal Page"

Date_____

"I will praise thee; for I am fearfully and wonderfully made" Psalm 139:14.

My full name	
My address	
My phone number	
My email address	
My height/weight	
When I was born	
Where I was born	
My brothers and sisters	
The places I have lived	
My fun activities	
Where I go to school	

Other information about me		A picture of me

"My Genealogy"

Write in the names of yourself, your parents and grandparents and other interesting facts about them (birthplace and date, who they were named after, occupation, date of death).

Me   **My parents**   **My grandparents**

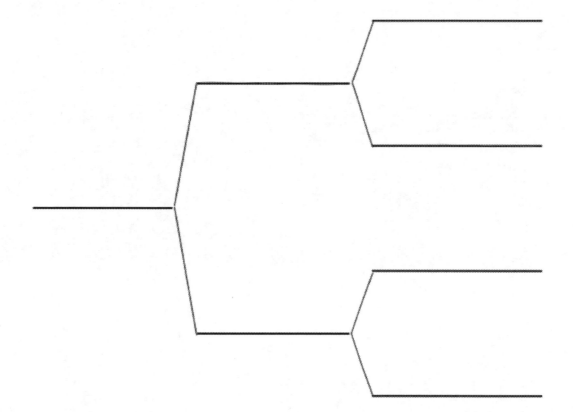

Other "interesting things about me"

Noah's Rainbow

Sower's Story

Fishermen's Ships

Jeremiah's Sash

Isaac's Sense of Smell

Gideon's Fleece

Jonah's Shade

Face of the Sky

House in a Storm

Ahaz's Sun Clock

Gideon's Thirsty Soldiers

Potter's Pots

Moon's Mission

Sound Senders

Elijah's Cloud

Gibeonites' Trick

Useful Salt

Weighing the World

Starry Sky

Bird's Eggs

STORIES WITH ACTIVITIES

Noah's Rainbow

Genesis 9:13-16

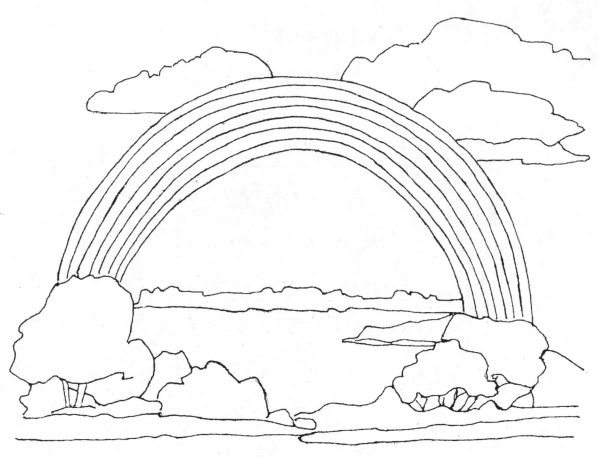

For accuracy, color after activity.

After the worldwide flood, God put a rainbow in the clouds of the sky. He told Noah that it was to be a reminder that He would never again destroy all living creatures in the world by a flood.

The rainbow is so beautiful that God has one around His throne, see Revelation 4:3. The colors of light are one of the most beautiful effects of science.

Colors of the Rainbow

Time: 30 minutes.

My test: Can I make a rainbow if I spray water in the air at the right position to the sun?

Items needed: Water hose with a strong stream of water, spray nozzle or your thumb, sunny day.

Procedure: Turn on the water all the way. With your back toward the sun, aim the hose up and spray the water to create a fine mist. Move around a little until you can see the colors.

Data: Color what you see. They should be in this order, red on top.

Red
Orange
Yellow
Green
Blue
Indigo
Violet

Conclusion: Rainbows are made by many small drops of water. Sunlight passes through these drops. The light rays of the sun are refracted (bent) by the water. The different colors of light separate because each color bends differently. The colors of the rainbow will *always* be in the order shown in Data. To help remember them, use the first letters of the colors, ROY G BIV.

Extra activity 1: Look for other things which spray water into the air, such as a fountain or waterfall. Observe the colors in the sunlight. Stand with the sun to your back, and move around until you can see the seven colors.

Extra activity 2: See the colors of light, the spectrum, with a water prism, found in "Light Shining" page 62.

Sower's Story

Luke 8:5-8

A farmer usually plants his seeds in rows (furrows) in prepared soil. Jesus told a story about a sower who planted his seeds by scattering them over the loose ground. That sower made the soil ready by loosening the dirt with a hoe or a plow. Then he took handfuls of seeds and threw them over the ground. Some seeds fell on hard ground instead of the good, prepared soil.

The seeds need the right conditions to sprout and grow up as plants. They need water, sunlight, and good soil. Then the healthy plants will bloom and produce food.

Jar Garden

Time: One month.

My test: Will seeds sprout and grow in the right conditions?

Items needed: Seeds of a vegetable (beans are good) or a flower, weed seeds, four large-mouth jars, paper, filler (cotton, peat moss, sawdust, or similar material), small rocks, and water.

Procedure: Prepare the jars by lining the insides with a layer of the paper. Fill the insides with the filler. Push six seeds between the paper and each jar. Label the jars according to the "conditions and jar number" in the Data chart. Keep the paper damp, but not standing in water, until plants that are still alive grow out of the jar. Plant those outside and continue to care for them.

Data: Record, with dates, what happens to the seeds.

Sowing seeds of the _____ plant Number of seeds in each jar _____ Date planted _____			
Conditions and jar number	What I do to this jar	Dates	What happened to my seeds
#1 Path Luke 8:5	I dump out the jar outside and I step on the seeds.		
#2 Rocks Luke 8:6	I put in seeds. I fill jar with rocks. Water only once.		
#3 Thorns Luke 8:7	I plant weeds with the seeds. Water to keep paper damp.		
#4 Good ground Luke 8:8	I plant seeds. Water to keep paper damp.		

Conclusions: When seeds have the right conditions they sprout.

Extra Activity: Continue to care for the plants until they have flowers and then more seeds. Draw your observations in "Plant Life Cycle" pages 70-71.

Fishermen's Ships

Luke 5:1-11

Simon Peter, James, and John were fishermen. They fished all night but didn't catch any fish in their nets. Jesus stepped into one ship to teach the crowd of people on the shore.

When Jesus finished teaching, He told Simon Peter to let down the nets again. They caught so many fish the nets broke. They filled both ships with so many fish that they began to sink.

Sinking Ships

Time: One hour.

My test: Boats and ships float on water, but if my ship is very full of cargo, will sink?

Items needed: Two paper boats for the ships (pattern in "Paper Boat or Box" pages 82-83); a pan or tub of water; some cargo—small blocks, coins, shells, beans, or beads.

Procedure: Float the ships on the water. Slowly put your cargo items in one of the ships, counting as you go. Continue until the ship sinks.

Data: Record the amount of cargo in smooth water.

	Empty ship	Full ship
Number of cargo items until ship sank	*Didn't sink*	

Conclusions: Too much cargo makes a ship float so low that water begins to flow into the ship. This causes the ship to sink.

Extra activity: On the Sea of Galilee storms often came up suddenly. "And there arose a great storm of wind, and the waves beat into the ship, so that it was now full [of water]" Mark 4:37.

My test: The ship will hold less cargo if there is a storm.

Procedure: Repeat the above activity of adding cargo, but this time churn (stir to make rough) the water with your hand.

Data: Record the amount of cargo in the rough water.

	Smooth water	Rough water
Number of cargo items until ship sank	(from first activity)	

Conclusion: Rough water causes the ship to list (tilt) side to side allowing water to splash into the boat. Too much water in the boat causes it to sink.

Jeremiah's Sash

Jeremiah 13:1-11

The Lord told Jeremiah to buy a linen sash (belt) and wear it next to his skin. He was not to wash it. Then he was told to go to the Euphrates River and hide the sash in a wet hole of a rock. After many days the Lord told Jeremiah to go back and dig up the sash. It was rotting and it was no longer useful.

Buried Cloth

Time: One month or more in hot weather.

My test: What will happen if I bury cloth in wet dirt?

Items needed: A strip of cotton or linen cloth (old shirt), about 3 inches (7cm) wide and 2 feet (60cm) long; a stream, a pond, or other wet area; a rock; a shovel.

Procedure: In Jeremiah 13, verses 1–7, God gives instructions to Jeremiah. Let's follow them.

- Get a cloth sash and wear it against your body. Don't wash it.
- Go bury the cloth sash under a rock next to some water.
- After many days go back and get the cloth.

Data: Write in what you did for each instruction.

Scripture— Jeremiah 13	What I Did	Results— What happened
Verse 2		
Verse 5		
Verse 7 "Many days"	Dug up cloth each week and checked condition of cloth until it began to decay and fall apart.	Week one - Week two - Week three - Week four - Week _____

Conclusion: The cotton cloth sash did become marred (damaged, rotten). It was no longer useful. The mold and mildew caused the fibers to break down, to rot and decay. Water allowed the mold and mildew to grow on the cloth. Worms and other animals might feed on the fibers, too.

Extra Activity: Bury other cloth of wool, linen, silk, and/or man-made fibers. Repeat the procedure above and compare how the fibers survived the wet dirt.

Isaac's Sense of Smell

Genesis 27:1-27

Isaac was an old man and could not see at all. But he could still smell and taste. Isaac asked his son Esau, a hunter, for some savory (good tasting) deer meat. Esau went out to hunt. Isaac's wife, Rebekah, heard what Isaac said. So she prepared some savory goat meat for their other son Jacob to take to his father.

Jacob tricked his father by pretending to be his brother Esau when he served the meat. Jacob put on Esau's clothing so that he smelled like Esau who often was outside in the wild. Isaac smelled Jacob's clothes to be sure it was Esau.

Smelly Clothes

Time: Half a day.

My test: Will a cloth which is dried outside smell cleaner than a cloth dried inside or a cloth not washed?

Items needed: Old dirty T-shirt, soapy water, and a sunny day.

Procedure: Cut or tear the T-shirt in three big pieces. Wash only one of the pieces in the soapy water and rinse. Put outside to dry in the sun. Put another piece outside to air in the sun. Leave the third piece indoors. Wait until the washed one is dry.

Now smell all three. Notice the difference among them. The father, Isaac, could smell a change when he smelled the clothes of his son Esau who loved to be outdoors and the clothes of his son Jacob who stayed indoors.

Data: Record how they smell to you.

Different cloths	How they smell
Dried outdoors in the sun	
Aired outside in the sun	
Left inside	

Results: The _____ smelled the cleanest.

Conclusion: The washed and sun-dried cloth smelled the cleanest. Most of the odors in dirty clothes come from the oils of our bodies. Soapy water loosens these oils. Heat from the sun helps these oils to evaporate into the outside air.

Extra activities: Smell your savory meat served at a meal. Now hold your nose closed with your fingers and take a bite, tasting with your tongue. How did it taste? _____. Now open your nose and take a bite and chew it. What is the difference? _____. So if you have to eat a food that doesn't taste good to you, just _____.

Gideon's Fleece

Judges 6:37-40

      God asked Gideon to go into battle to save Israel from their enemies. Gideon needed to strengthen his own faith and to encourage his soldiers before this great battle. So Gideon "put out a fleece," the wool skin of a sheep. One night Gideon asked God for a miracle, to let the dew "fall" that night on the fleece but not on the ground around it. The next morning he squeezed the dew out of the wool and got a bowl full of water. Then the next night Gideon asked God to keep the fleece dry and make the ground wet with dew that night. And that is what happened!

Wet Wool

Time: Two nights.

My test: Wool left on the ground overnight will be wet the next morning?

Items needed: A wool object (wool scarf or sweater or some yarn), an open area on a clear night, a measuring cup.

Procedure: On the first evening put the wool on the ground in an open area. In the morning feel the wool and the ground to determine if they are wet. If the wool is wet, squeeze out the water into a measuring cup and note the amount. Dry the wool during the day. The next clear evening put the wool out again.

Data: Mark (✔) in the proper boxes. Record any water.

First morning	Wet	Dry	Amount of water in wool
Wool			
Ground			
Second morning			
Wool			
Ground			

Results: Record what happened: _____

_____

Conclusions: Wet dewdrops form on any object that has cooled to the dew point, which is the temperature that water comes out of the air (condenses). It was God's sign or miracle that dew formed on the fleece but not on the ground. Then the next night dew formed on the ground but not the fleece. My fleece (wool) and the ground were wet each time, not like Gideon's.

Extra activity: Let dew collect on these materials, each about the same size. Which do you think will dry (water is gone) first? _____ Why? _____ Number order which they dried: paper____, glass____, cloth____, metal____, wood____, leaves____.

Jonah's Shade

Jonah 4:5-8

Jonah was out in the hot sun. He made a little booth or tent with a few branches to give him some shade from the sun. God gave him a big plant, a gourd, to grow over the booth. This cast a cooling shadow over Jonah and he was very glad. But when the plant died the next day, the sun beat down on Jonah's head. And he became angry and wished to die.

Sun and Shade

Time: One hour

My test: If I put animal fat in the shade, will it not melt as fast as the animal fat placed in the sun?

Items needed: Hot, sunny day; margarine, butter, bacon grease, or other animal fat; paper; ruler; booth or tent of a few branches in the sun; plants for dark shade; a watch or clock.

Procedure: Test the paper to see if it will absorb the fat. Rub some of the fat on the paper. Hold the paper up to the light. Is the rubbed spot brighter? _____. If "yes," then use this type of paper. If "no," try other types.

   Put a teaspoon (5 ml) of the fat on each of three pieces of paper. Place one paper in the booth, one in the shade of some plants, and the other one in full sun. Every 10 minutes measure the size of the fat spot on the paper. Repeat this three times.

Data: Record your measurements.

Size of Fat in Different Temperatures			
Time	Full sun	Booth	Dark shade
0 minutes			
10 minutes			
20 minutes			
30 minutes			

Results: The fat in the _____ melted the fastest. The fat in the _____ melted the slowest.

Conclusions: Heat causes the solid fat to become a liquid, or melt. The fat shows me (an indicator) what is hotter and cooler (temperature). The hotter the fat, the quicker it will melt.

Extra activity: If an outdoor thermometer is available, in each location measure the temperature and record the data.

Face of the Sky

Matthew 16:2-3

Luke 12:54-56

     The Israelites looked to the sky to guess what the weather would be like. When the sky was red in the evening, near sunset, they could expect the next day would be fair or clear. When the sky was very red with threatening clouds in the morning, near the sunrise in the east, they could expect the day to be stormy.

     When clouds began to rise out of the west, a rain shower was coming. To the west of Israel is a large sea with lots of water. When the winds began to blow from the south, they would be hot and dry winds from the deserts in southern Israel and southward.

Sky Watch

Time: Several days.

My test: Can I guess (forecast) the weather by observing the sky?

Items needed: None.

Procedure: Stand so that the sunrise is to your right, *east*, and the sunset is to your left, *west*. Then *north* will be in front of you and *south* behind you. Notice the colors of the sky and clouds.

Data: Record what you think weather will be like today and tomorrow (forecast) and what really happened.

What I am watching in the sky	What I think will happen today or tomorrow (my forecast)	What really happened
Sky color at sunrise in east		
Sky color at sunset in west		
Winds are coming from		
Clouds are moving from		
Amount of sky covered by clouds		

Conclusion: I can watch the sky and make a good guess (forecast) about what the weather will be. Weather is made by the sun's heat on the earth. It causes air to move and water to rise into the air forming clouds.

You can continue this study with "Elijah's Cloud" unit (pages 42-43) and "Clouds Types" (pages 60-61) and "Compass Directions" (pages 58-59).

Houses in a Storm

Matthew 7:24-27

Jesus told the story of two houses in a storm to describe a wise person and a foolish person. The wise person hears what Jesus says and obeys. He is like someone who builds his house on a solid rock. The rain falls and floods come and winds blow in a storm. They beat upon that house. But the house does not fall because its foundation is on a rock.

The foolish person hears what Jesus says and does not obey. He is like someone who builds his house on loose sand. The rain falls and floods come and winds blow in a storm. They beat upon that house. The house falls with a great crash because its foundation was on sand.

Building on Rock or Sand

Time: One hour.

My test: In a rainstorm will my model house on the solid foundation stand and the house on the loose foundation fall?

Items needed: Bucket or watering can, water, 4 blocks of wood for the house, a flat rock or cement block (larger than the house), pile of sand or loose dirt (larger than the house).

Procedure: Work in an area that can be wet and dirty. Stand the blocks of wood like a house on the rock or cement block. Fill the bucket with water and quickly pour it out like a river by the rock.

Next pile the sand into a hill and flatten its top. Place the block house on the sand. Pour a second bucket of water again quickly to flow past the hill.

Data: Draw the house and foundation before and after the water flowed past (the storm).

	House on rock	House on sand
Before the storm (water flow)		
After the storm (water flow)		

Results: The house on the rock _____

The house on the sand _____

Conclusions: The solid rock does not break apart after the water is poured. The rock supports the house. The loose sand or dirt does not hold together and washes away. The house falls because there is little to support it.

Ahaz's Sun Clock

Isaiah 38:8

King Ahaz noticed that the sun travels across the sky during the day. He built a way to tell time using the moving sun and stone steps - a sun clock or solar clock. At the top of the stairway was a pole to cast a shadow on the steps. When the sun was high in the sky, the shadow is short and only on a few steps. When the sun was low in the sky, the shadow was long and on many steps. The people could tell what time it was by looking at how many steps (also called degrees) had the pole's shadow on them.

In the Bible story of Hezekiah God made the shadow of the sun clock of Ahaz go backward instead of forward down the steps. This was a sign from God to King Hezekiah that he would get well from his sickness. You can read the entire story in 2 Kings 20:1–11.

Time with the Sun

Time: One day.

My test: Can I tell what time it is by the sun's shadow, just the way King Ahaz told time?

Items needed: A sunny day, a sunny location, a watch or clock, a ruler, lots of bricks or blocks, a pole or stick about 3 feet (1 meter).

Procedure: Stack the bricks or blocks like stairs with 12 steps, facing away from the sun. Use some of the bricks to prop up the stick at the top. Starting at noon, every 30 minutes adjust the bricks so that the shadow of the pole's tip falls right to the edge of the next brick or step. Measure the width of each step.

Data: Record the measurements of the afternoon shadow.

Time PM	Step number	Width in/cm of new step	Time PM	Step number	Width in/cm of new step
Noon	1		2:30		
12:30	2		3:00		
1:00			3:30		
1:30			4:00		
2:00			4:30		

Results: Each step measured the same (yes or no) _____.

Conclusion: I can tell time by the sun's shadow. I can see that the pole's shadow moves with the sun. The shadow goes forward (descends) the steps, showing the passage of time in the afternoon. By the number of steps I can figure about what time it is.

Extra activity 1: Observe your sun-clock steps in the morning, starting right after the sun comes up. Does the sun's shadow fall on them? _____. Did the shadow go forward (descend) or backward (ascend)? _____.

Extra activity 2: Look for other shadow changes during the day. Is there sunlight in your bedroom to make shadows? _____.

Gideon's Thirsty Soldiers

Judges 7:1-23

God asked a man named Gideon to gather an army of Israelites for battle against their enemy. Gideon gathered 32,000 men. But God wanted them to trust Him for the victory. So God told Gideon to take the thirsty soldiers to a stream to get a drink. God said that he should choose only those men who "lapped" the water to be in the fight.

Some of the soldiers went down on their knees, and putting their mouths in the water, sipped up what they needed. The others bent forward, and lifted the water with one hand and lapped the water into their mouths.

Three hundred men lapped the water and could watch for danger better.

Kneelers and Lappers

Time: One hour.

My test: To drink water will most of my friends kneel down and sip water from a bowl or scoop the water up with their hands to sip (lap)?

Items needed: Friends with washed hands; for each friend: a tub, pan or bowl of clean water, sword-like stick, and a cookie.

Procedure: Eat the cookies. Place the bowls full of water on the floor or ground in front of friends. Tell them to hold their stick and without touching the bowl quickly drink water for several seconds ("Ready, Set, Go"). Have their names in the Data chart.

Data: Record how friends drank the water.

Names of friends	Knelt down to sip up water	Lapped with hand to mouth	Other ways

Results: Add up the number of friends drinking each way.

Totals			

Conclusion: Most friends _____ to drink the water. Soldiers could better watch for danger by lapping.

Extra activity: Observe how animals drink water. Some animals sip, some lap. Birds dip their beak into the water then tilt their heads back. Wild animals must always watch for danger. Record the animal behaviors here.

Animals	How they drank water

Potter's Pots

Jeremiah 18:1–6

Jeremiah visited a potter's house. The potter made bowls, cups, pots, vases, and other earthenware vessels. The potter was stepping (treading) on the wet clay to get all the air bubbles out. Then he put the lump of clay in the middle of a flat wheel. He turned the wheel to spin the clay around as he shaped it. Jeremiah saw him mess up, so the potter mashed the clay into a lump again. The potter worked until he was pleased with his vessel. He marked a design on the jar. When dry, he baked it in a hot oven.

The potter may choose what he wants to make, a vessel of honor, like a pitcher to serve water, or a common (ordinary) vessel, like a pot for holding garbage. The apostle Paul compares God to being like a potter in Romans 9:21.

Making Pots

Time: Several days.

My test: Can I make a useful pot, jar, or vessel by working with wet clay, molding it, and then drying it?

Items needed: Clay* or paper-mache**, water, towel to wipe your hands, a flat surface to work on, a big stick, a sunny day.

Procedure: Wet the clay with some water. Throw the clay down over and over on the flat surface, or tread (step) on it, until all the air is out. Shape the clay into two pots, one to keep. Make a drawing of each step as you follow the procedures in Data.

Data and more procedures: Drawings of the pots in each step.

1. The two pots I have created.	2. Now mash one down.
3. Mold another pot from the mashed one.	4. Set the pots out in the sun until dry and hard.
5. Break one pot into big pieces (potsherds).	6. Now smash the pieces of these potsherds with the stick until they are like dust.

Conclusions: As a potter, I have control over my vessel. Clay is tiny grains of minerals. See "Rocks and Minerals" pages 64-65.

*Clay is often found under the topsoil layer.

**Use paper mache if clay is not available. Tear paper into small pieces and mix with a thick flour-and-water paste until very soggy.

Moon's Mission

Genesis 1:14, Psalm 81:3

The moon circles around our earth every 29 days. Early peoples used the moon to keep track of time. By observing the phases of the moon the time of month could be figured out. The new moon began the lunar month and was a holy day. People were sent to the top of a hill to look for this dark moon near the sun. When it was found, a trumpet was blown. Sacrifices were made and a delicious feast was held. It was a time of worship, as told in Numbers 10:10, Psalm 81:3, and Isaiah 66:23.

Moon Phases

Time: 1 month, mostly at night.

My observation: Can I see the moon with different amounts of light shining on it? The moon follows the same path as the sun, rising in the east and setting in the west.

Items needed: A clear sky on several days and a calendar.

Procedure: Observe the changes of the moon until it rises with the sun. Record that day and time, of the new moon, in the Data chart. View the moon a week apart (seven days) for a month. What time to look for the moon is given in the chart. Color the dark part black. If cloudy choose the next clear night.

Data: Chart of Moon Phases during month of _____

| Phases | Day and Time | Times moon is visible – | | What moon looked like |
		Rises in east	Sets in west	
New moon		Sunrise	Sunset	●
First quarter		Noon	Midnight	○
Full moon		Sunset	Sunrise	○
Last quarter		Midnight	Noon	○

Notice at full moon, the moon looks fully lighted for four nights.

Extra activity: If binoculars or a telescope are available, look at the moon. See the craters and hills. The height of the hills can be seen where the light and dark parts of the moon meet.

Sound Senders

Isaiah 44:23

All the things in God's creation seem to sing. It seems like they are rejoicing because God made them. When we are thankful, even the hills and mountains seem to sing. The trees make sounds like they are clapping their hands with joy, Isaiah 55:12. The skies have sound in the thunder, Psalm 77:18. Waves of water lift up their voice, Psalm 93:3-4.

Humans can hear sounds that vibrate within a certain range of high and low pitched sounds. Some animals can hear much higher or lower pitched sounds than we can.

Sounds Around

Time: 15 minutes. (However, you may continue to listen.)

My observation: By listening carefully, can I hear many sounds made by the things in God's creation? Are sounds different according to the time of day or night?

Items needed: None.

Procedure: Listen to the sounds of nature (other than humans) - water, storms, animals, and even plants that are around you. Write down what made the sound, what the noise was like, and how loud it was. Listen carefully to birds. They may have a caw, chirp, squawk, trill, quack, hoot, or other noise, as in Psalm 104:12.

Data: Record sound observations in this chart.

Time of day	What made the sound?	What was the noise like?	Other observations:

Results: Most of the sounds I heard were made by _____.

Extra activity: The sounds that we hear are the vibrations in the air that reach our ears. Find out how different sounds are made.

Our voice is the sound produced by the vibration of the vocal cords in our throat. A grasshopper rubs his legs together. A frog fills an air sack under his throat to make a croak. Dry seeds in a dry pod or gourd rattle. Two branches on a tree rubbing together can make a groaning sound. Lightning heats air causing it to expand, then when the air cools, it rushes back with a bang called thunder. Others: _____

Elijah's Cloud

1 Kings 18:41-46

    This is a description of the changes that happen to water. Elijah's servant looked toward the sea. A lot of water had evaporated from the sea. This water vapor soared high into the air, though no one could see it. Elijah prayed and the vapor cooled and condensed (came close together) to form water droplets. They collected into a cloud. The cloud got bigger and other clouds formed. The clouds became dark with so much water the sunlight couldn't get through. The water droplets became big and heavy. They precipitated (fell) to the earth in a great rain storm.

    Another description of God making rain is in Job 36:27-28.

A Drop's Trip

Time: One day.

My observation: Can I recognize the changes of a drop of water and follow its cycle?

Items needed: A pond or lake and a day when it rains.

Procedure: Water drops evaporate (escape) as a gas (vapor) from lakes and other bodies of water. Water drops also transpire (escape) in the breath from animals and from plant leaves. Breathe on your hand and feel the moisture.

The water vapor travels up in the air until it cools and becomes a little liquid drop again. This is called condensation. Many little drops collect together to make clouds. Find clouds in your sky or fog near the ground.

The water cycle continues as the water drops become bigger and heavier until they fall as rain. This is called precipitation. If the air is very cold, the water drops fall as snow. (See "Snowflakes" pages 80-81.)

Data: In the diagram below, draw pictures of places your drop travels on its trip.

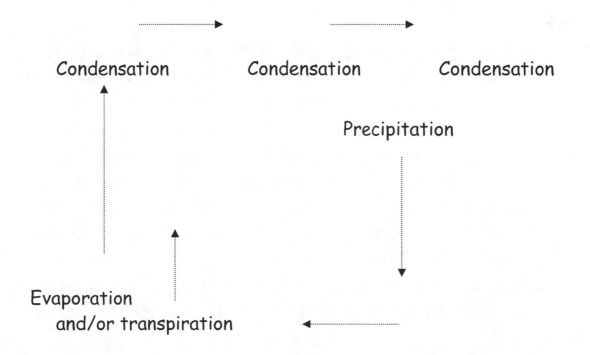

Gibeonites' Trick

Joshua 9:3–27

God told the Israelite leader Joshua to destroy all the people in Canaan because of their wicked living. The people of the city of Gibeon wanted to make peace with Joshua so that the Israelites would not kill them. They lived only a few miles from where the Israelites were camped. They decided to fool the Israelites, pretending that they lived in a far away country.

This is how they tricked Joshua and his men. They put on ragged clothes and worn out shoes. They carried dry, moldy bread and torn wineskins. When they went to visit the Israelite camp, they acted as if they were very tired from a very long journey. The Gibeonites were very good actors and the Israelites believed them.

Moldy Bread

Time: Two weeks.

My test: What happens to bread when it gets older?

Items needed: Two pieces of homemade bread, biscuit, or pancakes; and two airtight containers.

Procedure: Take pieces and put each in an airtight wrapping. Put one in a cold place and the other at room temperature. Leave for at least two weeks. Look at both pieces every day to see if there are any black or green spots of mold or other happenings.

Data: Record when mold first appears. After two weeks, write a summary of your observations, such as dryness, color, odor, and the amount of mold.

Breads	Date mold appears	Observations at two weeks
Covered bread, room temperature		
Covered bread, cold temperature		

Conclusions: Cold temperature slows down the formation of mold.

Extra activity: Compare homemade bread slices left uncovered inside your house and outside your house in a dry place.

Which slice do you think will develop mold first? _____.
Did any animals eat some of your bread? _____. Did both slices become dry and hard? _____. What else did you observe?

_____

Warning: Some molds are *bad* – can cause sickness; some are *good* – used to make certain cheeses or the medicine penicillin.

46

Useful Salt

Matthew 5:13

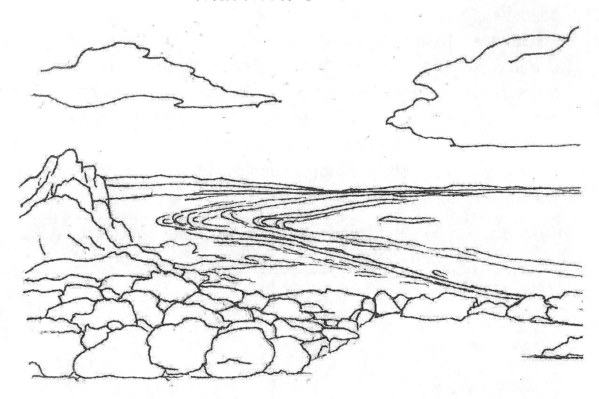

    Salt in Bible times, as well as today, is used to season food to add more flavor. However, we can ruin the flavor of food if we put too much salt on it. Salt can keep bacteria from growing. Salt can keep some foods from spoiling. God commanded the Israelites to put some salt on the sacrifices that they burned on the altar in the Temple.

    Salt is plentiful around the Dead Sea in Israel. They call it the Salt Sea, even though it is a lake. The water that flows into the lake evaporates, leaving the minerals or salts behind.

    Salt becomes impure if mixed with sand. It can lose its flavor when left out in damp weather. It is worthless. It cannot become salty again.

Salt Crystals

Time: One to two weeks. Start date _____, end date _____.

My observation: When salt water (brine) loses its water, are salt crystals are left behind?

Items needed: A 2 quart (2 liter) glass bowl, 1 cup (240 ml) of fresh warm water, table salt, and a tablespoon (15 ml spoon).

Procedure: Stir 4 tablespoons (60 ml) of salt into the water until most of the salt is dissolved. Allow the bowl to sit without moving until the water is gone. A warm, dry place is best.

Data: Draw what some of your crystals at the bottom of your bowl look like. If you have a magnifying lens it will help you see the shape. Taste one of the crystals. What does it taste like on your tongue? _____.

Results: There is a difference in crystal shape on the sides of the bowl and on the bottom. Those on the sides evaporated faster so the molecules of salt didn't have much time to form the cubic shape. The crystals on the bottom grew slower and have a more perfect shape. (See drawings of Dead Sea salt around the Table of Contents pages 5 and 7.)

Extra activity: Grow salt crystals from different kinds of salt: rock salt (mined), sea salt (evaporated), or other salt. Follow the same procedure as above.

Extra activity: Water two weed plants each day with water for a week. Water one with 1/2 cup (120 ml) of fresh water and the other weed with 1/2 cup (120 ml) of salt water, 1 teaspoon (5 ml) of salt added to the water. Observe what happens to the two plants. _____

Weighing the World

Jeremiah 10:12, 51:15

Scripture says God made three areas to our world. By His power He made the *earth* or geosphere, which includes the nonliving things of our planet Earth, such as rocks and soil. By His wisdom He made the *world* or biosphere, which includes all living organisms, plants and animals. By His discretion (understanding) He made the *heavens*, which refer to the Earth's atmosphere that surrounds the Earth and to the astrosphere or outer space including the stars. God has stretched out the heavens and no telescope can see how far that is.

Scale for Weighing

Time: One hour.

My observation: Can a balance scale weigh a sample of God's creation?

Items needed: A measuring stick or other straight stick; two paper cups; string; weights - coins, beans, pebbles, or beads of the same weight; water; and soil.

Procedure: Make a simple balance scale according to the diagram. This is similar to how merchants weighed produce in Bible times.

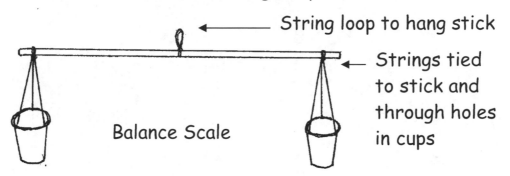

String loop to hang stick

Strings tied to stick and through holes in cups

Balance Scale

Balance the stick with the two empty cups so that the stick is level. This is your first measurement – air. Then add water to almost fill one cup. Add weights to the other cup until the stick is level again. Record the number of weights it took. Empty the water and repeat procedure with the soil (dirt).

Data: Record findings on chart.

Weighing cup items	Number of weights in measuring cup	Results
Air	0	*Air in my cup doesn't seem to have any weight*
Water		
Soil		

A span is the distance of a stretched hand from thumb tip to little finger tip. Even God weighs and measures, Isaiah 40:12.

Starry Sky

Psalms 8:1, 3; 19:1-6   Job 9:9

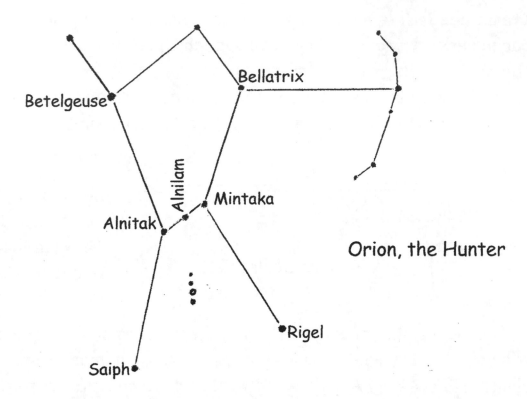

Orion, the Hunter

The heavens above will never cease to declare the majesty and glory of God. The sun, moon, and stars speak to us and to God, praising Him, Psalm 148:3. "Their line is gone out" is the light that shines into the entire world from these heavenly bodies. As we look out from our planet into the sky we see a vast universe out there sprinkled with stars and galaxies too numerous to count. God has counted and named them, Psalm 147:4. Man has named some of the stars, and groups of stars called constellations.

The sun comes up beaming like a bridegroom and marches across the sky like a king with his servant stars. The sun runs the same race every day. The sun's light also has solar heat. Nothing on planet Earth is hid from the heat of the sun. Our star, the Sun, has a diameter of 870,000 miles (1.4 million kilometers) and has a surface temperature of 11,000°F (6000°C).

Build a Constellation Model

Time: One hour or more.

My observation: In the constellation Orion, the Hunter, are stars really different distances away from Earth and are different sizes even though they may look the same?

Items needed: A ruler; string; 7 cotton balls or beads; glue or tape; scissors; and a box, turned on its side, to hang the "stars" - at least 15 inches (38 cm) wide, 12 inches (30 cm) deep, and 15 inches (38 cm) high.

Procedure: Using the measurements given, construct a model of the constellation Orion. Punch a hole on top of the box at each measurement (right and front). Tape or glue the strings from each hole with the balls or beads hanging the proper length.

Stars	Measure from right	Measure from front	Length of string	*Solar diameter
Betelgeuse	13 3/4 in. (35 cm.)	1 1/2 in. (4 cm.)	2 in. (5 cm.)	650
Rigel	3 3/4 in. (9.5 cm.)	4 1/2 in. (11.5 cm.)	13 1/2 in. (34.5 cm.)	70
Bellatrix	6 1/4 in. (16 cm.)	1 1/2 in. (4 cm.)	2 3/4 in. (7 cm.)	6
Mintaka (double star)	8 in. (20 cm.)	10 3/4 in. (27.5 cm.)	7 3/4 in. (19.5 cm.)	60
Alnilam	9 in. (23 cm.)	5 1/2 in. (14 cm.)	8 1/2 in. (21.5 cm.)	65
Alnitak	10 1/4 in. (26 cm.)	5 in. (13 cm.)	9 in. (23 cm.)	60
Saiph	12 in. (30.5 cm.)	1/2 in. (1.5 cm.)	14 3/4 in. (37.5cm.)	11

Results: From the front, the model of the stars should look like the constellation Orion the way we see it from Earth.

*Solar diameter number tells how many times to multiply it with our Sun's diameter, 870,000 miles (1.4 million km.), to find the star's size.

Bird's Eggs

Deuteronomy 22:6-7

Man has been given dominion over the "fowl of the air", the birds. We are to care for His creation. He gives us permission in the above verse to take the bird's eggs but not the mother bird. Nests can be found in trees; in rocks, Jeremiah 48:28; and even on the ground, like the ostrich's nest, Job 39:13-15. The sparrow and swallow could be found nesting around the house of God, Psalm 84:3.

Birds were valuable in Israel to feed on snakes and scorpions, insects, mice and other small animals, thus keeping them under control. Birds were also used in the Jewish religious rituals.

Egg Legs

Time: Half an hour.

My test: How strong is a bird's eggshell that protects the baby bird? Is it possible to use eggshells as legs for a plant stand?

Items needed: Chicken eggs, scissors, tape, short piece of wood board or plastic (like a CD case) and a small potted plant.

Procedure: To make eggshell halves, wrap two pieces of tape around the middle of an egg, leaving a tiny space. Tap along the space with a sharp edge, breaking the shell. Gently pull apart (catch the egg yoke and white for cooking).

Even up the shell's edges with the scissors. Place the shells, edge down and dome up, for the four corners of the board. Put the board on top the egg domes. Place the potted plant on top.

Data: Draw in the space what your plant stand looks like now.

Results: The eggshells became legs for the plant stand and could hold up the weight. The eggshell's dome is a strong shape.

Notice that an egg has a dome on each end, shaped a little differently. Why? _____.

Extra activity: Does acid rain from air pollution affect eggshells of baby birds? Eggshells are made of calcium, as is the enamel of our teeth. Calcium reacts with acid. Sin reacts in us in a bad way.

Procedure: Take a piece of your eggshell or whole egg and tie a string around it. Hang the shell in a jar or glass from a stick laid across the top. Repeat for each liquid to test. In each glass cover the eggshell with one liquid acid - vinegar, soft drink (especially cola drinks), old milk, or fruit juice. Tap water (from faucet) and rain water could be compared. Write what each liquid is on labels taped to each glass.

Each day check the shell's hardness and other observations. Which eggshells were softened more quickly? _____.

"My Notes"

(Experiments, ideas, drawings, etc.)

Magnify His Work

Compass Directions

Cloud Types

Light Shining

Land Features

Rocks and Minerals

Animal Homes

Leaves

Plant Life Cycle

Tree Bark

Fingerprints

Singing

NATURE STUDY

Magnify His Work

"...I will gather all nations and tongues; and they shall come, and see My glory" Isaiah 66:18.

"Remember that thou magnify His work, which men behold. Every man may see it; man may behold it afar off" Job 36:24-25.

God has encouraged us to take a close look at His creation, His work. We can see the stars far off. We can see the plants and animals and rocks around us. But take a closer look, really close. Observe the detail in His creation.

Activity: Make a magnifying lens using a drop of water, a liquid lens. By looking through the water drop the object will appear larger. To practice magnifying: write your name on a small piece of paper. Look at it through the water drop. Raise or lower the drop until the letters are in focus (a sharp, clear image).

Look at parts of God's creation, such as a feather, tiny flower, rock, your fingerprint, drop of pond water, and other interesting things.

Step 1: *Water drop in a loop of wire -* Take a paper clip or short length of wire and bend it to make a loop about 1/8 inch (3 mm) or a little larger. Dip 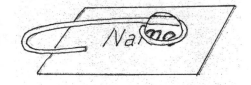 your finger in water to collect a drop. Place this drop on the loop. Now hold the loop over the letters of your name.

Step 2: *Water drop in hole of stiff paper or card –* Cut a card about 4 inches (10 cm) long and 1 1/4 inch (3 cm) wide. Punch or cut a hole about 1/5 inches (.5 cm). Place a drop of water on the hole. Look through the drop. If the card soaks up the water, 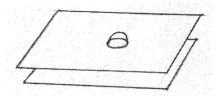 then put a small piece of tape over the hole. Place the drop over the hole on the tape. Now look at the letters of your name and see the difference in size.

Step 3: *Water drop on plastic wrap* - Take a small piece of clear plastic wrap or clear sticky tape and place a drop of water on it. Look through the drop at your letters. Try different sizes of drops and measure them (place the wrap with drops over the ruler). Which drop size worked the best to magnify your name? _____ .

Step 4: Which method magnified the objects the best for you?

_____ .

Step 5: Now enjoy "magnifying His works" with your magnifier. Use other magnifiers if you can locate them, such as a larger magnifying lens, microscope, binoculars, or telescope. Cameras have lenses too. With a computer and a webcam or digital camera, objects can be magnified.

Other magnifying activities:

Plastic bag and water magnifier – Add some water to a small, clear plastic bag. Close bag tightly (a Ziploc-type bag is easiest to use) and look through it at an object. Try different amounts of water. More water magnifies _____ .

Plastic bag and air magnifier – Fill small, clear plastic bag with air. Hold the bag partly in a clear dish of water. Look at an object under the dish through the bag. Did this method magnify the object? _____ .

Other liquids – Use a drop of other clear liquids, such as mineral oil (like baby oil) or rubbing alcohol. How do these liquids compare to water for magnification? _____ .

Two magnifiers together – Hold two magnifiers or lenses so that you can look through both at the same time. How does this change the image? _____ .

Compass Directions

"And thou shalt set the table without the vail [veil], and the candle-stick over against the table on the side of the tabernacle toward the south: and thou shalt put the table on the north side" Exodus 26:35.

"And they [Gentiles] shall come from the east, and from the west, from the north, and from the south, and shall sit down in the kingdom of God" Luke 13:29.

This is a map's compass rose. It shows directions on a map. The compass rose looks a little like the petals of a rose. Map makers wanted a pretty way to show all directions. Most maps are drawn with north at the top. See the compass rose on the Israel map (page 124).

Activity: Try different ways you can find north, south, east, and west directions without a compass.

Step 1: *Sun and Moon* - These two big lights in the sky seem to rise in the eastern direction and set in the western direction. Our earth is actually turning towards the east as it spins. Stand so that your right side is toward the east (sunrise) and your left side is toward the west (sunset). Now you are facing north with south behind you.

Step 2: *Shadow-tip compass* - Find a straight stick about 3 feet (1 meter) long and a clear area in sunlight. Push the stick in the ground straight up. Place a small stone at the tip of the shadow cast by the stick.

Observe the tip move until about 2 inches (5 cm) away from the stone. Mark the tip of the stick's shadow with another small stone. Draw a line starting from the first mark through the second mark about 12 inches (30 cm) long. Stand with your left foot on the first mark and your right foot at the end of the line drawn. North of the equator you will be facing north. South of the equator you will be facing south.

Step 3: *Stars* - The North Star is always visible in a clear sky north of the equator. Two bright constellations move around it. Look for them. They point to Polaris, the North Star, and the end of the Little Dipper's handle.

Big Dipper   **Little Dipper**   **Cassiopeia**

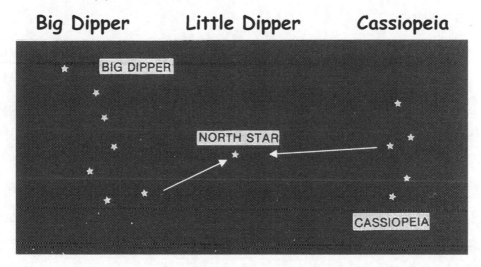

Step 4: *Magnet* - Gather a small magnet and a sewing needle or thin iron nail. Hold one end of the needle or nail. With the magnet stroke it in one direction, toward the other end, a dozen times.

Take 12 inches (30 cm) of thin string and tie the middle of the needle so that it balances (hangs level). Hold the other end of the string and observe the needle turn north (or south). Is the needle point or the needle eye pointing north? _____.

Or float your needle on water. Very carefully lay the dry needle on top of some water in a clear dish. You may also place the needle on something floating on the water, like a little piece of paper or cork. The magnetized needle will turn north (or south). (Keep the needle from touching the side of the dish.)

Cut out the paper protractor (page 125) and place it under the dish. Turn the protractor until 0°/180° lines up with the north/south needle. Now you can easily tell the other directions.

Cloud Types

"Look unto the heavens, and see; and behold the clouds which are higher than thou" Job 35:5.

"With clouds He [God] covereth the light; and commandeth it not to shine by the cloud that cometh betwixt" Job 36:32.

God creates clouds from evaporated water. Clouds are in the air around the earth. They can be very high, thin ice clouds. They can be very low, thick fog. Clouds can be stormy or beautiful colors and shapes.

Activity: Become aware of the clouds in the sky. Notice how different they are. Notice they may be moving across the sky or becoming a different shape. Pick a thin or small puffy cloud and observe it for a few minutes to see if it moves, changes shape, or becomes a different color.

Step 1: Study these basic types of clouds on the next page. Learn their names and at what height in the sky they are found.
Step 2: Look for these clouds. Observe how they cover the sun. Observe their shapes.
Step 3: Draw some of the different clouds you see and label them using the chart. Of course, there are many more cloud types and it is interesting to learn about them.

I saw these cloud types_____.

Cloud Types

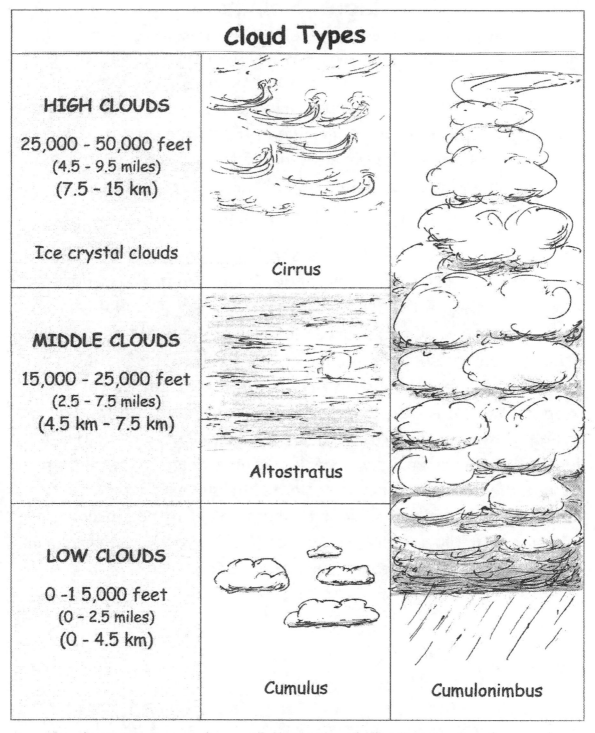

HIGH CLOUDS 25,000 - 50,000 feet (4.5 - 9.5 miles) (7.5 – 15 km) Ice crystal clouds	Cirrus	
MIDDLE CLOUDS 15,000 - 25,000 feet (2.5 - 7.5 miles) (4.5 km – 7.5 km)	Altostratus	
LOW CLOUDS 0 -1 5,000 feet (0 - 2.5 miles) (0 - 4.5 km)	Cumulus	Cumulonimbus

Cloud names are made up of these words (with meanings):

alto – high   **cirrus** – curl   **cumulus** – heaps, piles

nimbus – rainstorm   **stratus** – spread out, layer

Light Shining

"By his [leviathan] neesings [sneezing or snorting] a light doth shine...out of his mouth go burning lamps, and sparks of fire leap out...he maketh a path to shine after him" Job 41:18-19, 32.

This Scripture is a picture of a fierce leviathan (dinosaur or sea dragon) splashing and swimming in the water with the light of the sun sparkling on the water. Read of the sun shining on grass after a rain in 2 Samuel 23:4 and lightning in Job 38:24.

Activity: Ways to observe sunlight on a bright sunny day.

Step 1: Look at leaves or flowers in the bright sun and compare with similar leaves or flowers in the shade. What do you observe about the color of the two? _____. Notice the shade plants are dull and darker in color without the direct light.

Step 2: Look at sunlight shining on splashing water. Notice how the water sparkles like little fires, as in the Scripture verse.

Step 3: Make a *water prism* that separates light into the colors of light, the spectrum, as in a rainbow. Set a tray in bright sunlight. Fill with water. Lean a small mirror against an inside edge. Adjust the mirror so that it reflects the sun onto a piece of paper. Color bands will shine in brilliant colors of red, orange, yellow, green, blue, indigo, and violet (ROY G BIV). The spectrum will always be in this order. Can you see each color?

Water Prism

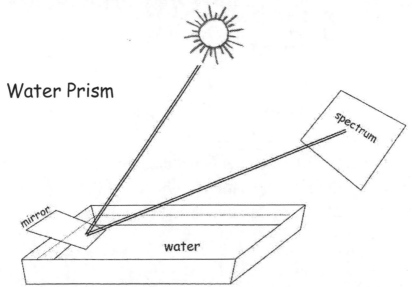

Do not look directly at the sun or its reflection! It may damage your eyes.

Land Features

The Lord said, "Turn you, and take your journey...unto all the places nigh thereunto, in the plain, in the hills, and in the vale, and in the south, and by the sea side...unto the great river, the river Euphrates" Deuteronomy 1:7.

There are quite a number of physical features of the land in the Bible. God created a wide variety on the crust of our Earth.

Activity: How many of these features can you find around you?

Step 1: Look at the list of land features below and record the description of those land features, if you have them in your area.

Land feature	Descriptions of land features	Scripture	Happenings in Scripture
Brook or river		1 Samuel 17:40	
Lake		Luke 8:22	
Valley		Genesis 26:19	
Plain	*Flat land with no trees*	1 Kings 7:46	
Hill		Matthew 5:14	
Mountain		Micah 7:12	
Others:			

Step 2: Look up the Scriptures and record what was happening at that land feature. Read more verses for the whole story.

Step 3: Become aware of the many other variations of land that are mentioned in the Bible, like islands, marsh, desert, and caves. There is a map of Israel in the Appendix (page 124). A satellite photo of Israel and the surrounding countries is on the back cover of this book. Notice the different features of the land.

Rocks and Minerals

"And between the passages...there was a sharp rock on the one side, and a sharp rock on the other side" 1 Samuel 14:4.

"That they [Job's words] were graven with an iron pen and [filled in with] lead in the rock for ever!" Job 19:24.

"And He [Jesus] answered and said unto them, 'I tell you that, if these [the multitude of people] should hold their peace, the stones would immediately cry out'" Luke 19:40. Rock crystals and metals are in satellites, radios, and other sound systems.

Minerals are the chemicals that make up rocks and stones. The Bible mentions the minerals gold, silver, copper, lead, tin, and iron. They have unique properties, features that are special to them. Many gems and precious stones are mentioned in the Bible, such as those attached to the breastplate of the priest, Exodus 28:17-21. Rocks are a source of metals and gems for jewelry; building material for walls of houses, bridges, and other structures; metals for tools, utensils, and weapons.

Activity: Test some rocks in your area for the properties on the chart. There are more properties you may want to learn about and test. The acid vinegar's reaction to rocks of calcium is exciting.

Step 1: Gather different kinds of small rocks to test.

Step 2: Test your rocks' properties and place each rock on the chart where it belongs. You may not be able to find all of those on the chart.

Step 3: If you know the name of the rock or mineral write it in the blocks. Or write a short description of the rock.

Step 4: Look up other Scriptures about rocks, metals, and gems.

- 1 Samuel 7:12 – Samuel set up a stone and called it "Ebenezer", which means "the stone of help". This was to remember how the Lord helped them in battle.
- Genesis 28:11, 18 – Jacob took a stone for a pillow.
- Revelation 21:18-21 – The Holy City, made of precious stones.
- _____

Properties of Rocks and Minerals Test		
Hardness Leaves a scratch in the rock	Soft – scratch with copper coin	Medium – use iron nail	Hard – use steel file
Color	White	Other colors	Black
	quartz		
Luster How light reflects from rock	Earthy – dull	Glassy	Brilliant – sparkles
Streak Drag rock across a rough white surface	No color	Yellow, pink, or light gray	Dark gray or black color
Fracture How it breaks	Very small	Uneven	Sharp
	clay		

Animal Homes

"And Jesus said unto him, Foxes have holes, and birds of the air have nests; but the Son of man hath not where to lay his head" Matthew 8:20, Luke 9:58.

"...Strong is thy dwellingplace, and thou puttest thy nest in a rock" Numbers 24:21.

Animals live in many different types of homes. Often they are near their source of food and water. Sometimes they stay in their home all during the winter when there is little food available.

Activity: Observe the type of home an animal has – web, nest, hole, or other shelter. Observe the animal's activity around it.

Step 1: Choose an animal to study. It could be a spider, bird, lizard, frog, snake, snail, turtle, sheep, goat, cow, horse, insect, or worm, all of which are mentioned in the Bible.

Step 2: Spend time observing your animal—_____. Does it live alone or with others? _____. Does your animal have a home? _____. Does your animal build its home, like a spider web or bird nest? _____. Do humans provide the home, like a barn for sheep or horses? _____.

Step 3: Does your animal use the home in bad weather? _____. Does your animal rest/sleep there or just raise their young in the home? _____.

Step 4: How does your animal get its food? _____ _____. Does the home help, like a spider's web that catches insects? _____.

Step 5: What danger does your animal face? _____. Does its home protect it from those dangers? _____.

Step 6: Draw a picture of your animal and its habitat. Write a poem. Or write a little play or skit and act out your animal using its home, from what you have learned.

Step 7: Thank God for the home you have to live in. What does your home do for you? _____

_____.

Leaves

"And the dove came in to him [Noah] in the evening; and, lo, in her mouth was an olive leaf pluckt off" Genesis 8:11.

"Now learn a parable of the fig tree; When her branch is yet tender, and putteth forth leaves, ye know that summer is near" Mark 13:28.

The Bible mentions many plants and they all have leaves, from the tall cedars of Lebanon to the prickly thistle. Find leaves that look similar to them in your area.

Activity: Look at the different leaves of plants in the Bible in the chart below. Match them with leaves you can find around you. If possible, find out the name of the plants you found.

Step 1: Study the type and shape of these leaves.

Biblical plant leaves with a Scripture		
Single leaf type	**Compound leaf type**	**Heart shape**
Olive	Lentils	Grape
Genesis 8:11	2 Samuel 17:28	Numbers 13:23
Needle or scales	**Three lobes shape**	**Many lobes shape**
Cedar of Lebanon	Fig	Melon
Ezekiel 31:3	Proverbs 27:18	Numbers 11:5

Step 2: Collect leaves to match these types and shapes. It may be a different plant that has a similar leaf. Draw what your leaf looks like in this chart. Write the name of the plant in the space under the leaf if you find out what it is.

Single leaf type	Compound leaf type

Heart shape	Needle or scales shape

Three lobes shape	Many lobes shape

Step 3: Notice some other features of the leaves –
Margins (edges): Smooth, teeth, and/or lobes.
Tips and bases: Pointed, rounded, truncated (straight).
Veins: Palmate   pinnate

Is the leaf surface smooth or hairy? _____. Do the veins of
the leaf stand out? _____. What color is the leaf? _____.
Do the leaves drop off in the winter time? _____. Observe
how the leaf is attached to the plant.

   Some leaves are used for food, like lettuce and spinach.
Some leaves are used for medicine, Ezekiel 47:12, like sage. Some
are poisonous, like poison ivy, and will irritate skin.

Step 4: Do a rubbing of a leaf. Lay the leaf with the raised veins
up. Put a thin piece of paper over the leaf and rub all over with
the side of a crayon or charcoal. Be sure to rub the leaf margins.

Step 5: Press your leaves between the pages of a heavy book. In
a week or so the leaves should be dry.

Step 6: Observe leaves even closer with a magnifying lens or
microscope. Can you find any chewed areas, eggs, or fungus? _____.

Plant Life Cycle

"For the earth bringeth forth fruit of herself; first the blade, then the ear, after that the full corn [or grain] in the ear [or head]" Mark 4:28.

Living organisms have a life cycle. Most plants begin from a seed in the ground. Mark 4:26–29 gives a good example of the life cycle of a corn or grain plant.

Activity: This activity is different from the others as it will take a few months. From your jar garden, in the "Sower's Story" unit (page 17), plant several sprouts in good soil. Care for them with water and sun. Draw and label one plant in the different stages of its life cycle.

Life Cycle of a _____ **Plant**

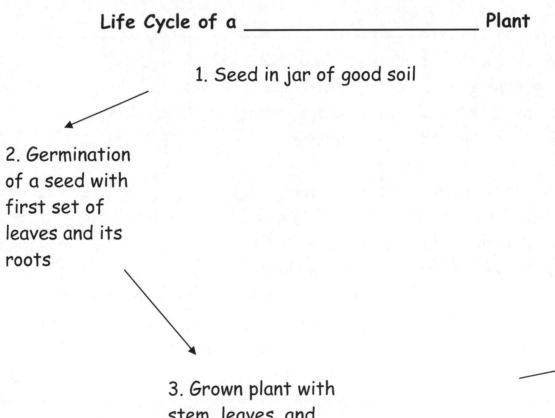

1. Seed in jar of good soil

2. Germination of a seed with first set of leaves and its roots

3. Grown plant with stem, leaves, and flower buds

6. Open fruit showing
arrangement of seeds

7. Dead plant with dry
 or rotten fruit

5. Plant stem with fruit

 4. Flower –
Top view

Side view

Tree Bark

"The cedars in the garden of God could not hide him: the fir trees were not like his boughs, and the chestnut trees were not like his branches; nor any tree in the garden of God was like unto him in his beauty" Ezekiel 31:8.

"Moreover the word of the Lord came unto me, saying, Jeremiah, what seest thou? And I said, I see a rod of an almond tree" Jeremiah 1:11.

Trees have an outside covering of plant tissue called bark. It protects the moist wood behind it that carries the food and water from the tree's roots. Bark also protects the tree from insects, disease, and temperatures that are very hot or very cold.

The dead, thick bark must expand as the tree grows. This stretching creates bark that has patterns, such as furrowed (ridges), scaly, shaggy, or papery. Some ridges are sharp and some flat. Some trees shed their bark regularly.

Activity: Make a bark rubbing collection to compare the differences in tree barks.

Step 1: Gather thin paper (like newsprint) and wax crayons (peeled) or charcoal.

Step 2: Choose trees with different patterns of bark. The trunks of the trees will show more ridges than the branches.

Step 3: Hold or tape the paper over the bark. Gently rub the side of the crayon or charcoal all over the paper. Use enough pressure to show the high parts but not punch holes.

Step 4: If you know the name of the tree, write it on the paper. Record the color of the bark and any other features, like flaky.

Step 5: Do at least five rubbings to start with. Group your rubbings by patterns – furrowed, scaly, shaggy, papery, or other.

Step 6: Look for injuries by insects, birds, storms, or humans. Look at how the marred bark heals itself around an injury.

Step 7: Observe the trees around you with a sharper eye. Notice the trunk bark may be different at different heights. Branch bark is usually different from the trunk bark.

Some Tree Bark Patterns

Shallow, irregular furrows Sweet Gum	**Smooth but blotchy bark** Crape Myrtle	**Rough, scaly plates** Pine
Strongly furrowed Black Walnut	**Regular blocks** Persimmon	**Large, branched thorns** Honey Locust

Below is one of my rubbings and what I observed about this bark.

Fingerprints

"Thine eyes did see my substance, yet being unperfect; and in thy book all my members were written, which in continuance were fashioned, when as yet there was none of them" Psalm 139:16.

When we were being formed, fashioned, in our mother's womb, God had already planned, "in thy book all my members were written", just what we would look like. No two people are exactly alike, although we have the same members: eyes, ears, hands, and feet. For example, everyone's fingerprints are a little different.

Activity: Make a set of your fingerprints and classify them.

Step 1: Gather materials: pencil, paper or card, clear sticky tape.
Step 2: Make an "ink" pad by rubbing the pencil over a small area of the paper or a card, making it a black pencil smudge.
Step 3: Press and slightly roll a finger's first joint in the smudge.
Step 4: "Lift" the print by placing a short piece of sticky tape over your blackened finger. Carefully pull off the tape and stick it in its proper box.

Right hand (first joint of each finger) of _____ (name)

Thumb	Pointer	Middle	Ring	Little

Left hand (first joint of each finger) of _____ (name)

Thumb	Pointer	Middle	Ring	Little

Step 5: Now classify the patterns of each print according to the illustrations. These are the three basic types of ridge patterns. Record the pattern name in the box under each print. Use a magnifying lens or water drop (see "Magnify His Work" pages 56-57), to make it easier to see your prints.

Loop	Whorl	Arch

Step 6: Which of your fingers have similar patterns?
Whorls _____
Arches _____
Loops _____

Step 7: Compare your fingerprints with a friend's fingerprints. Are any exactly alike? _____. The patterns of ridges on our finger pads are unique.

Extra activity: Make prints of your whole hand (fingers and palm) or your whole foot. Dip in thin mud, wet clay, paint, or finger paint (flour and water paste with coloring of powdered paint or dyes). Press onto paper or wood. Or leave print in a thick layer of mud or clay, like an animal leaves its tracks.

Another activity: Dust for a latent (invisible) fingerprint. On a glass surface make a fingerprint by rubbing a finger on your nose then pressing your finger on the glass. Dust the print gently with a feather or a very soft brush dipped in cocoa or other dark powder. "Lift" the print by pressing clear sticky tape over it then stick the tape in this box. Label pattern of the fingerprint.

Singing

"O sing unto the Lord a new song: sing unto the Lord, all the earth" Psalm 96:1.

"Now therefore write ye this song for you, and teach it [to] the children of Israel" Deuteronomy 31:19.

One of the easiest ways to learn Scripture is by putting the verses to music and singing them. One way to observe nature with a keener sense is to make up a song about what you are observing.

Activity: Study an animal or plant.
Write a song about its life, behavior, and appearance. Songs are poems put to music. Use a tune you already know for the music. Or make up your own tune.

Step 1: Choose one animal or plant: _____.
Step 2: Write down *descriptions* of it after spending time carefully observing it. Below are some suggestions of what to look for:

Animal – Life: gathering and eating food, communicating, sounds, grooming, resting, and shelter. Appearance: skin covering (feathers, fur, scales, hair), color, wings or arms/legs, and head. Its function: pet, pest, food, beauty.

Plant – Life: tree, bush, grass, vine, or flower; type of fruit; where found; who eats it. Appearance: color of leaves, type of flower, way it grows. Its function: food, beauty, protection.
My observations -

Step 3: Write down *feelings* you have about the animal or plant.

Step 4: Write your song. Usually each word syllable has a musical note. Choose a method:

- Hum a tune but change the words using your descriptions and feelings. Write down the tune's name and your poem. Sing it over and over, changing the word arrangement until it flows well.
- Write short sentences with lots of descriptive words and feelings, creating a poem. Rearrange the order of the words if you want it to rhyme. Then find a tune that seems to fit the flow.
- Create your own music for your poem. Write the music down so that others can play it. Write the words under the notes.

Step 5: Neatly write a final copy. Include the title of your song, the poem, and the name of the tune you are using, if not your own.

Step 6: Decorate with related drawings or items glued on.
Step 7: Sing it! Such wondrous things of nature the Lord has made! There are many Scripture verses about singing, such as, "Make a joyful noise unto the Lord, all the earth: make a loud noise, and rejoice, and sing praise" Psalm 98:4.

"My Notes"

(Experiments, ideas, drawings, etc.)

Snowflakes

Paper Boat or Box

Scavenger Project

Fishing Nets

Weaving

Wave Your Flag

Messing with Clay

CRAFTS FROM THE BIBLE

Snowflakes

"Hast thou entered into the treasures of the snow?" Job 38:22.

Snow is made of tiny frozen crystals of water.  They form when water vapor (gas) condenses into ice (solid). Most snowflakes are hexagons with six sides or points. Most are symmetrical, meaning one side looks the same as the other. Every snowflake is a little different, unique just like we are.

Activity: Make an original paper snowflake, one of a kind.

Step 1: Gather scissors and square sheets of paper.

Step 2: Fold the paper diagonally.   Now fold again.

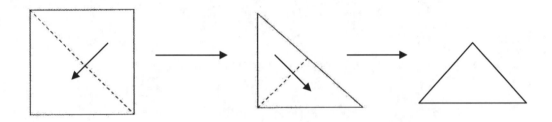

Step 3: Now fold into thirds (two folds).

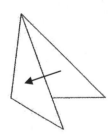

Step 4: Cut off bottom points.

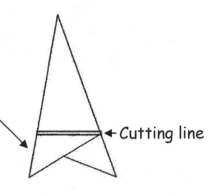

← Cutting line

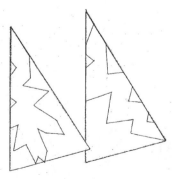

Step 5: Cut out parts of the sides (see examples). Don't cut through some edges.

Step 6: Open the folds and observe the snowflake you created. Some flakes are very fine, fern like. Others are bold and thick. What kind did you make? _____.

Step 7: Create another snowflake. Make it smaller and different. Stick it here on your paper.

Step 8: If you live in an area where it snows, study snowflakes as they fall using a magnifying lens or a cold microscope outside. Or create your own snow storm by making more paper snowflakes and hanging them around your room.

Paper Boat or Box

People who faced storms in a boat - Jonah (Jonah 1), Jesus' disciples (Matthew 8:24; 14:24 and Mark 4:37), and Paul (Acts 27).

Fishing boats and cargo ships were often small. They were wooden with sails to catch the wind. They faced many storms on the open water. King Solomon had a navy, a fleet of ships, 1 Kings 9:26, 10:22. Baby Moses floated in an ark of reeds, Exodus 2:3-5.

Activity: Origami or paper folding is one way to make a little floating boat, or a box to hold little things. Using half a sheet of paper, fold it to make a boat or box. Test your boat.

Step 1: Cut an 8½ x 11 inch (22 cm x 28 cm) or similar size paper in half to make an 8½ inch x 5½ inch (about 22 cm x 14 cm) piece.

Step 2: Crease paper into thirds. *(look at the bottom of the page)

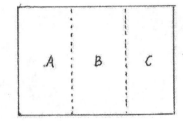

The dashed lines are folds.
The solid lines are edges. Write in the letters to understand the folding.

Step 3: Fold C over B, then A over C. Then crease this in half lengthwise.

Step 4: Fold A to the left. With C, fold over the four corners, meeting in the middle to make D and E.

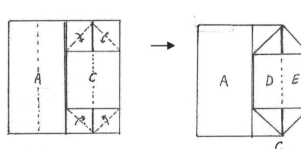

*A measure for thirds of your paper.

| 1/3 | ↑ | 1/3 | ↑ | 1/3 |

Step 5: Next fold D over E.

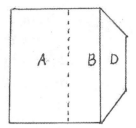

Fold A over B and D.

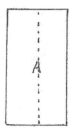

Step 6: Fold down corners of A

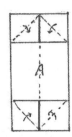

to make

$\longrightarrow$

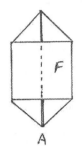

Step 7: Fold F to the left to show D again.

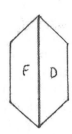

Step 8: Gently pull apart at the centerline of FD to make a flat-bottomed **boat**, with the ends curved upward.

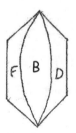

Step 9: Test the boat by floating in smooth water. Now stir up the water and float your boat in "stormy" water. (See "Sinking Ships" page 19.)

Step 10: Gently squeeze the ends of the boat toward each other until it is **box** shaped. Crease sharply all the corners and bottom edges.

Extra: Try different papers or cards for the boat or the box.

Extra: Make two boxes, one slightly smaller than the other. Fit together as top and bottom boxes.

Scavenger Project

"And the earth brought forth grass, and herb yielding seed after his [its] kind, and the tree yielding fruit, whose seed was in itself, after his kind: and God saw that it was good" Genesis 1:12.

"And one went out into the field to gather herbs, and found a wild vine, and gathered thereof wild gourds his lap full…" 2 Kings 4:39.

What an awesome creation we live in. God created such a wide variety of plants and animals. What is in your area that you would like to collect and display? _____.
Be careful not to collect live animals or poisonous plants or fruits.

Activity: Scavenge or hunt for natural items around you that you could put together to make a wreath, mobile, table decoration, collage, jewelry, weaving (see "Weaving" pages 88-89) or other science/art project. Have a theme, such as different textures, color, uses, or other creative ideas. Display or use your project.

Step 1: Decide what project you would like to do and your theme.

Project _____ Theme _____

Step 2: Take a container and go out, scavenging for items of God's creation. Here are some ideas:

Seeds, grains	Bark, twigs, vines	Feathers, fur, hair
Nuts, acorns	Grasses or reeds	Shells
Cones, balls, pods	Moss, lichens	Old nests
Dried berries, vegetables and fruits	Dried flowers, ferns, leaves	Rocks of different kinds and sizes

Other items:

Step 3: Bring back your collection and plan how to use it. Now that you have your items, your project may be different from your original idea. That's OK, as you needed a starting point.

Step 4: Select your base or background to put items on. Ideas – clay, twigs, wood, bark, leather, rock, cardboard, thin metal, wire.

Step 5: Stick, tie, wire, or glue (hot glue only with adult super-vision) items from your collection in a pleasing arrangement. Look at it from different angles and distances.
What is your project theme? _____.

Step 6: Your finished project could be sprayed with a clear lacquer or gold paint (great for Christmas). Ribbon or a small figurine (a small carved or molded figure of an animal, angel, etc.) could be added. Other ideas - _____

Step 7: What did you learn about your environment from your scavenged collection?

Step 8: What did you learn about one of God's creations in your collection?

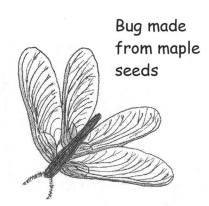

Bug made from maple seeds

Step 9: If you did another scavenger project, what would you do differently?

Fishing Nets

Fishermen using and mending their fishing nets, Matthew 4:18-22.

"...'Launch out into the deep, and let down your nets for a draught' [catch]...And when they had this done, they enclosed a great multitude of fishes: and their net brake" Luke 5:4, 6.

Several types of fishing nets were used in Bible times. The cast net was a circle flung into shallow water. The dragnet was large and took two boats to drag it through the deep sea for fish. (See illustration in "Fishermen's Ships" page 18.) The full nets were brought to shore and the fish taken out. Then the nets were spread out on rock to dry and be mended. The fishermen made and repaired their own nets. Tears in the net would let fish escape through the holes.

What net cords (fibers) would be strong for a long time in the water when fishing? An experiment is in "Additional Activity" on the next page.

Activity: Make a simple net or mesh wall hanging.

Step 1: Gather materials needed – stick or rod about 10 inches (25 cm) long; cord or twine, 37 feet (11.3 meters); and scissors.

Step 2: Cut 12 lengths of cord 3 feet (90 cm) long. Save the extra foot (30 cm) for the end. Tie each cord on a stick with Lark's Head knots, as shown. Hold both ends of the stick in place by having a friend hold it, tying to a chair, or your creative way.

Lark's Head knots

Overhand knots

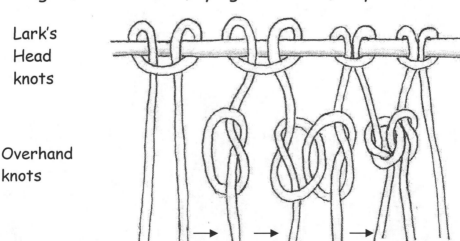

Step 3: Tie two tight Overhand knots together (see Step 2) every 1 inch (2.5 cm) following the diagram. Continue to the end of the cords.

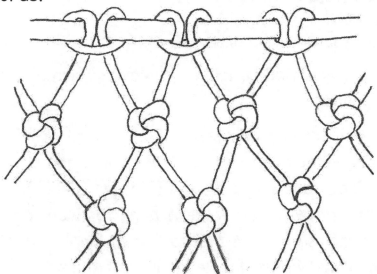

Step 4: To end the net, use the extra cord. Cut into three 4" (10 cm) pieces. Tightly tie every four cords together near the ends. Trim ends evenly.

Step 5: Display your net. What fibers did you use? _____.

Additional activity: Take several short strings or cords of different fibers. Cut each in half, and label all of them (cotton, hemp, or whatever you have). Keep one set dry. Soak the other set in water. Do you think water will weaken the fibers? _____. After a few days, test the dry cords and wet cords by pulling on them. What happened? Make a chart to show your results.

88

Weaving

Yarn was spun, Exodus 35:25.
Fabric woven for the tabernacle, Exodus 35:35.
Fine linen was brought from Egypt, Ezekiel 27:7.
Linen was made from flax, Isaiah 19:9.
The warp and woof are mentioned in Leviticus 13.

Activity: Make a woven wall hanging by weaving yarn and native plants you have collected.

Step 1: Gather materials – yarn, string, or cord of any fibers; two small tree branches or sticks for the frame; and dry plants to weave (for ideas see "Scavenger Project" pages 84-85).

Step 2: Study the drawing on the next page for weaving suggestions. For the frame, cut two branches the width you want your hanging. For the *warp* (vertical or lengthwise fibers), cut lengths of the yarn, string, or cord three times as long as you want your hanging. (The extra third length is needed for the knots.) Lay out your plant collection in a pleasing arrangement with a variety of widths and shapes, colors, spaces, and textures.

Step 3: Tie a row of Lark's Head knots (see "Fishing Nets" pages 86-87) along the top branch, keeping the ends even. Tie another cord to the ends of this branch for hanging while working and when finished.

Step 4: Tie the end of each cord over the bottom branch with a knot.

These warp cords are now ready for weaving.

Half Hitch   Two Half Hitches

Step 5: Hang your frame from the top cord. Tie a weight (such as a rock, glass bead, or ball of clay) on each end of the bottom branch to keep the warp tight. The weights could be left on your finished work if desired.

Step 6: The *woof* or *weft* (horizontal or filling fibers) will be the plants you have gathered. Start at the top and weave over and under the warp cords, as illustrated. You could skip warp cords for a different effect. Keep the rows snug against each other unless you want an open weave. A fork or large comb helps to slide the plants together.

Step 7: Display your beautiful weaving from God's creation.

Example of a weaving:

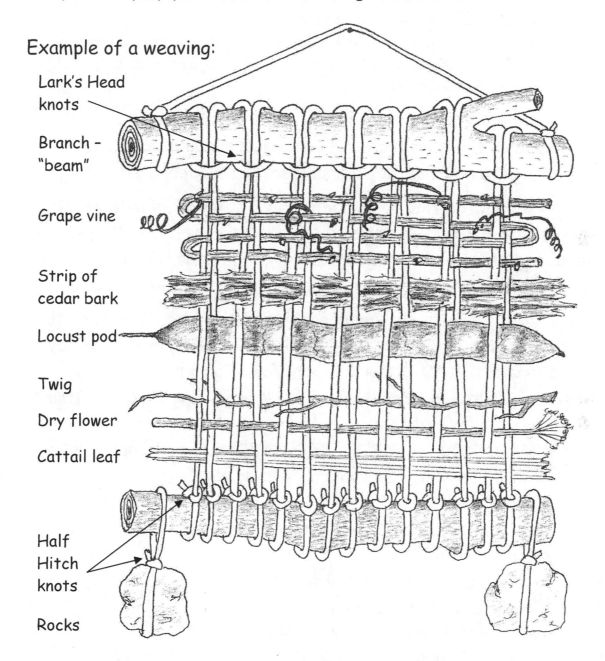

Lark's Head knots

Branch – "beam"

Grape vine

Strip of cedar bark

Locust pod

Twig

Dry flower

Cattail leaf

Half Hitch knots

Rocks

To weave fabric, the warp yarn is strung between two weaver's beams. The woof yarn is wrapped around a *shuttle*. This smooth, straight stick is run back and forth through the warp.

Wave Your Flag

"And the children of Israel shall pitch their tents, every man by his own camp, and every man by his own standard [flag], throughout their hosts" Numbers 1:52.

"Thou hast given a banner [flag] to them that fear thee, that it may be displayed because of the truth" Psalm 60:4.

"And the Lord their God shall save them in that day as the flock of His people: for they shall be as the stones of a crown, lifted up as an ensign [flag] upon His land" Zechariah 9:16.

The Hebrews in the wilderness had standards (flags) to identify each tribe. Armies carried banners or ensigns (flags). These flags were colorfully embroidered and decorated.

Activity: Create a flag to symbolize you. It could include your family name, your given name, a skill you have (for example, you play a musical instrument or are involved in an athletic activity), a goal you have, a motto, and other symbols to represent you.

Step 1: Gather supplies – plain fabric for the flag, about 12"x16" (30 cm x 40 cm) or larger; paper and pencil; paint, dyes (see "Dye Fabric" pages 106-107), markers, and/or crayons; glue; beads, stickers, pictures, nature items; a stick for a flag pole; and string. Decorate your flag so that it could fly in wet weather?

Step 2: Sketch out your ideas on paper. Dividing the paper into sections will help. Keep it simple. See example.

Step 3: Color your final flag plan in the colors you want to use. You will not be able to erase on the fabric.

Step 4: Start at the top of the flag fabric and work down so that you will not smear any marks or knock off any glued items.

Step 5: When finished, back away and study your flag to see if there is anything that needs improving and make the changes.

Step 6: Proudly display your flag.

Messing with Clay

"And the Lord God formed man of the dust of the ground, and breathed into his nostrils the breath of life..." Genesis 2:7.

"...I also am formed out of the clay" Job 33:6.

"...how are they esteemed as earthen pitchers, the work of the hands of the potter" Lamintations 4:2.

Clay was easily available and widely used – for bricks, mortar, writing tablets, seals for letters and doors, pottery and molds for pouring melted metals. Even we are made of the elements of the dust of the ground, which includes clay. See "Rocks and Minerals" pages 64-65.

Activity: Make items from clay. Some ideas are vessels (bowl, dish, pot, pitcher, and vase, see "Making Pots" page 37), hot plate, tile, brick, beads and other jewelry pieces.

Step 1: Can you find clay under the topsoil or near a creek in your area? If not, buy clay or a clay substitute. Locate a place with a flat work area and one that can be wet with water. Wear an apron or smock and have a towel handy. You may want to use tools, such as a stick or wire loop for carving clay, a wire or thin stick for making holes in beads, and a potter's wheel.

Step 2: If using real clay, wet it and throw it down over and over to force any air bubbles out. Mess around with the clay - roll long strands of clay, roll little balls, flatten clay. Have fun!

Step 3: Make something to use. The flattened clay could be shaped into a leaf for a dish. The long strands could be coiled around and around to make a vase, or use a potter's wheel, if available, to make a vase. Carve a design in a clay piece. If you mess up, mash the clay together and start over.

Step 4: Dry your piece in the sun. It will probably take several days. Paint it if desired. The pottery is fragile unless baked (fired) in a hot fire or kiln. When fired, a chemical change takes place in the clay to make it hard, waterproof, but not break proof.

"My Notes"

(Experiments, ideas, drawings, etc.)

Build a Fire

Bake Breads

Cook a Stew

Catch, Clean, and Cook a Fish

Take a Hike

Graft a Branch

Make Paper

Dye Fabric

Sandals

ACTIVITIES WITH ADULTS

94

Build a Fire

"Then shall it be for a man to burn: for he will take thereof, and warm himself; yea, he kindleth it, and baketh bread" Isaiah 44:14-15.

"And the sons of Aaron the priest shall put fire upon the altar, and lay the wood in order upon the fire" Leviticus 1:7.

Fires were necessary for cooking, warmth, light, and for religious sacrifices. Fires can be both useful and dangerous. They must be carefully tended to. Fire in the Scriptures was used to symbolize God's presence and His judgments.

Activity: Learn to build a fire, cook with it, and put it out properly. Fires need three things – heat, oxygen, and fuel.

Step 1: Unless in an indoor fireplace, locate a safe place at least 6 feet (2 meters) clear away from buildings, trees, and other things that could catch on fire. A pit could be dug in the ground for the fire, especially on a windy day.

Step 2: Gather firewood and place it within your reach. Stack in separate piles. Cover wood when not in use to keep it dry.

- *tinder* (shredded bark, dead pine needles and other dry leaves, cones, thin dead branches and _____)
- *kindling* (sticks your finger width or smaller)
- *fuel* (large wood, split if needed)

Have matches, and a candle for easier lighting. Fill a bucket or pot with water for your fire bucket, and have it within reach if needed to control the fire.

Step 3: Now sketch a simple map of your cook fire layout. Include the fire area, fire bucket, woodpile, chopping area, table, and any seats.

Step 4: To "lay a fire" first determine the wind direction for the oxygen needed for your flame.

For a *lean-to,* put your tinder next to a log on the side the wind is from. Rest the kindling over the tinder against the log.

For a *tepee* or *cone,* lay the kindling over the tinder as shown.

Touch a lighted match or candle to the tinder. Hold until tinder has flames.

Step 5: Care for your flame by adding kindling until the fire is strong enough for the fuel to catch fire. Feed it gently; don't smother it. Let the fire burn long enough to make some hot coals before starting your cooking. It is easier to control the temperature with coals than flames.

Step 6: Cook your food – boiling in a pot (be sure to soap the outside first for easier cleaning), baking in a Dutch oven or reflector oven, roasting on a spit or grill, or frying in oil in a pan. Rocks or logs could be used to support your cooking pots. Type of cooking used _____. Food cooked _____.

Step 7: Enjoy your food and the warmth and light of the fire. Never leave the fire without someone caring for it. Sparks and flames could get out of control with a sudden gust of wind.

Step 8: Put out the fire thoroughly. Sprinkle the fire with water by splashing water with your hand from the fire bucket. Use a stick to turn over any smoldering wood. Continue adding water until there is no more smoke. Cover the coals with dirt and place a short stick straight up in the middle of the dead fire for location.

Step 9: What did you learn from this activity?

Warning - Never build a fire without a responsible adult's permission and supervision. Fires can be very dangerous, causing destruction and even death.

96

Bake Breads

"In the sweat of thy face shalt thou eat bread, till thou return unto the ground..." Genesis 3:19.

"Take thou also unto thee wheat, and barley, and beans, and lentils, and millet, and fitches [spelt], and put them in one vessel, and make thee bread thereof..." Ezekiel 4:9.

"It is like leaven, which a woman took and hid in three measures of meal, till the whole was leavened" Luke 13:21.

Bread was the most important food in Bible times. It was made from a variety of finely ground grains (flour). Bread was baked in fireplaces, clay ovens, or even on hot stones or coals.

Leaven was fermented bread dough saved in a clay vessel from the last bread, like our sourdough today. It was added to the next batch of bread. The leaven produces air that expands when heated, causing the bread to rise.

Activity 1: Bake flat, *unleavened bread*.

Step 1: Bread ingredients:
> 1 cup (240 ml) wheat or other flour
> 1/8 teaspoon (.5 ml) salt
> 1 tablespoon (15 ml) vegetable oil
> 1/4 cup (60 ml) cool water (more if crumbly)

Step 2: Pour oil into water. Add this to flour and salt. Mix until it forms a ball of dough that pulls away from the side of the bowl.

Step 3: Knead on a floured board or in a plastic bag until smooth. Let dough rest 15 minutes.

Step 4: Form into 4 small balls, 1 1/2 inches (4 cm). Save one ball for the next activity. Roll or stretch each ball until thin and about 5 inches (12 cm) in diameter.

Step 5: Place on hot, dry skillet. Toast over medium heat until brown spots begin appearing, about 2 to 3 minutes on each side.

Step 6: Draw a picture of your unleavened flat bread.

Step 7: Enjoy eating your unleavened bread.

Activity 2: Now make some *leavened bread.*

Step 1: To make sourdough leaven, take one of the balls of dough and add enough warm water to make soupy dough. This will become your "starter." Add a tablespoon (15 ml) of honey to feed it. Leave lightly covered in a warm place for a day. Add equal amounts of flour and water to make 1/2 cup (120 ml) of the starter. Leave overnight to work (ferment). It should smell strong.

Step 2: Add starter to 1 1/2 cups (360 ml) of flour, 1/2 teaspoon (2.5 ml) salt, and 1 cup (240 ml) water.

Step 3: Combine all ingredients. Cover with a damp cloth and let rise, doubling in size, in a warm location for several hours. Shape into a round loaf and place on a pan. Rise again in a warm oven, 100°F to 150°F (37°C to 65°C), for 2 hours.

Step 4: Preheat oven to 325°F (162°C). Place loaf in oven and bake for half hour or until golden brown.

Step 5: Draw a picture of your leavened sourdough bread.

Step 6: How is it different from the unleavened bread in height, texture, and taste? _____

_____.

Step 7: Enjoy eating your leavened bread. Try spreading it with soft cheese (curdled milk) or honey and butter (churned milk).

Cook a Stew

"And Jacob sod [boiled] pottage [stew]; and Esau came from the field, and he was faint...Then Jacob gave Esau bread and pottage of lentils..." Genesis 25:29, 34.

"And one went out into the field to gather herbs, and found a wild vine, and gathered thereof wild gourds his lap full, and came and shred them into the pot of pottage [stew]: for they knew them not" 2 Kings 4:39.

Stews were a common form of food. A large pot stood over a fire and small pieces of meat, rice or meal, and vegetables were boiled slowly for the evening meal. The Hebrews planted gardens of herbs (vegetables) which included onions, leeks, garlic, beans, lentils, greens, cucumbers, and seasonings/spices for the stews. Sometimes they found wild foods to add to the pot, but they could get sick if they didn't know what the plants were.

Activity: Cook a stew for your family or friends. Serve with your bread and a drink - milk, grape juice, or tea.

Step 1: Here is a suggestion for a stew recipe to serve 6 or more.

2 cups (.5 liter) lentils

6 cups (1.5 liters) water

1 tablespoon (15 ml) olive oil

1 large onion, chopped

2 carrots, sliced or chopped

1 lb. (400 g) of chopped cooked lean meat or fish (optional)

1 teaspoon (5 ml) salt

Other vegetables and grains, such as tomatoes, rice, barley, beans, or whatever is available in a garden

Good sprinkling of seasonings/spices, such as parsley, mint, garlic, dill, cumin, or others you like

Step 2: Gather ingredients and put in a large pot. Cover and cook slowly over your fire. Stir often and add water, if water evaporates. Cook until all is tender, at least half an hour. Smells good and great flavor!

Step 3: Serve and enjoy. How would you change the stew?

Catch, Clean, and Cook a Fish

"And the other disciples came in a little ship...dragging the net with fishes. As soon then as they were come to land, they saw a fire of coals there, and fish laid thereon, and bread" John 21:8-9.

"But ask now the beasts, and they shall teach thee; and the fowls of the air, and they shall tell thee: Or speak to the earth, and it shall teach thee: and the fishes of the sea shall declare unto thee" Job 12:7-8.

There are many references to fishing and eating fish (especially tilapia) as it was a staple food for the Hebrews in the Sea of Galilee region. We are to have dominion over fish, Genesis 1:26. We can learn about the animals God created by studying a fish.

Activity: Catch and clean a fish. Observe the main parts of a fish, outside and inside, its anatomy. Cook and eat your fish.

Step 1: Catch a fish at least the size of your hand. Use hook and line or a net. Where and how did you catch your fish? _____
_____. If you are in an area where it is not possible to catch a fish, go to the market and buy a fish. Ask for one that has not been cleaned.

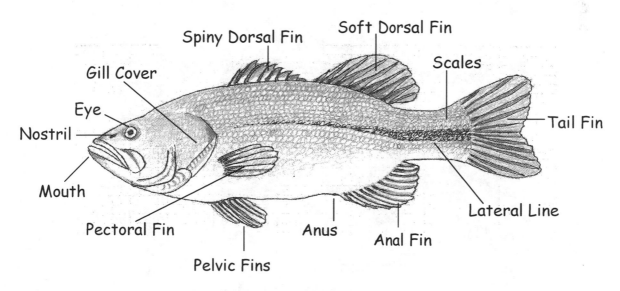

External Fish Anatomy

Step 2: Study the outside of your fish and draw what it looks like. Label according to the external anatomy diagram.

How do fish move in the water? _____

How do they get their food? _____

How do they protect themselves? _____

Step 3: Clean the fish. First scale the fish by scraping the skin with a knife from the tail forward to the head. Then cut off the head behind the gills. Slit open the belly to the anal fin. Study the inside anatomy, finding the main parts.

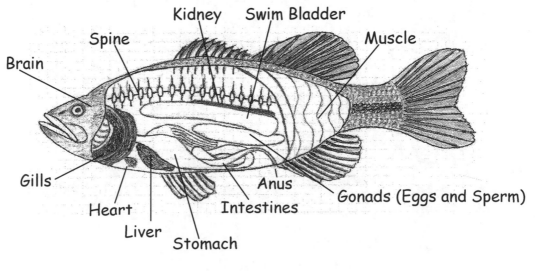

Internal Fish Anatomy

Step 4: Compare the insides (internal organs) of the fish with your internal organs. What things are similar? For example, you and a fish both have a stomach and _____.

What organs are different? For example, you have lungs and a fish has gills, _____

Step 5: Draw what your fish looks like inside. Label according to the internal anatomy diagram.

Pull out the inside organs and throw in trash. Wash out the cavity thoroughly.

Step 6: Cook your fish – bake, broil, grill, fry, poach (boil in liquid), or add to stew. Cook until it flakes easily when pricked with a fork. Smells good and great flavor!
You and your adult cooked the fish by _____
_____

Step 7: Eat your fish. Yumm!
What did you like about your fish activity? _____
_____

What would you do differently on your next fishing adventure?
_____

Take a Hike

"And Jesus entered into Jerusalem...and now the eventide [evening] was come, He went out unto Bethany with the twelve" Mark 11:11.

"Now Bethany was nigh unto Jerusalem, about fifteen furlongs off" John 11:18.

Jesus and His disciples often traveled between Jerusalem and Bethany, a distance of about two miles. They walked on the dusty, rocky road wearing sandals.

Activity: Plan a *day hike* of about two miles (3 km), on a dirt road or trail if possible. Have an adult with you and some other friends (Jesus had at least twelve). Wear sandals or go barefoot if your feet are tough enough.

JAARS Road Map

Step 1: Study a map of the hiking area, such as a camp, recreational park, ball field, beach, or other public areas. Figure the distance out and back or a continuous, circular trip. Plan when and where to meet to start the hike.

Step 2: Be prepared. Take along plenty of drinking water. Other suggested items to take are a snack, map, compass, hiking stick, bandana, magnifying lens, paper and pencil for observations, Ziploc-type bag for collecting, and small first-aid kit. Carry things in your pocket, backpack, or fanny pack. This leaves your hands free for your hiking stick and to study things.

Step 3: On the day of the hike check the weather for rain and temperature. Dress properly and in layers (several shirts/coats). Be sure everyone has permission to go. Have fun!

Step 4: As you walk be observant of your surroundings – plant and animal life, weather, noises, smells, and unexpected things. Be aware of yourself – how do your feet feel; have you had a drink of water lately; are you too hot or too cold; do you need to rest?

Step 5: What did you learn from the hike? Share your thoughts.

Additional activity: Go on a *night hike*. What differences do you notice, such as color, sounds, smells, and other changes?

Graft a Branch

"For if thou wert [were] cut out of the olive tree which is wild by nature, and wert graffed [grafted] contrary to nature into a good olive tree: how much more shall these, which be the natural branches, be graffed into their own olive tree?" Romans 11:24.

Grafting takes two living plants and unites them so that they grow as one plant. To graft plants, take one variety producing good fruits and another variety producing good roots. Normally a good fruit tree branch is grafted onto the good root tree, but in the Bible verse a wild fruit branch is grafted in.

Activity: Use the "whip" grafting method to grow two plants together. Use two varieties of growing vegetable plants, like tomatoes; or fruit plants, like grapes; or flowers, like geraniums.

Step 1: Choose the strongest plant to be the "stock" that has the root growing in soil. This plant will receive the "scion" (a twig or shoot) from the other vegetable or fruit plant. The scion should be about the same diameter (thickness) as the stock.

Step 2: Cut the stock above the ground. With a knife split the stock one inch (2.5 cm).

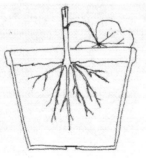

Step 3: Cut the end of the scion in a V or wedge shape.

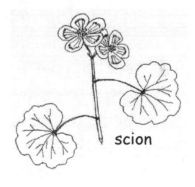

scion

Step 4: Slip the scion into the stock.

scion

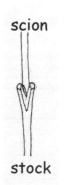

stock

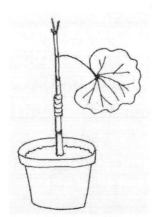

Step 5: Wrap snuggly with stretchable tape. Trim most of the leaves. Keep the soil moist. When the scion sends out new leaves, carefully remove the tape.

Make Paper

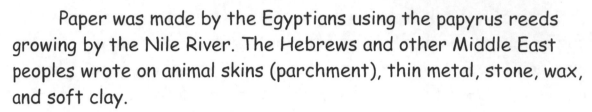

"And the Lord said unto Moses, 'Write this for a memorial in a book...'" Exodus 17:14.

"...Baruch wrote from the mouth of Jeremiah all the words of the Lord...upon a roll [scroll] of a book" Jeremiah 36:4.

Paper was made by the Egyptians using the papyrus reeds growing by the Nile River. The Hebrews and other Middle East peoples wrote on animal skins (parchment), thin metal, stone, wax, and soft clay.

Activity: Make a paper scroll from several sheets of paper you have made. The paper will be made from recycled wood fibers, wastepaper. Experiment with other plant and animal fibers until you find the look and feel of the paper you like.

Step 1: Collect equipment needed to make paper –
- blender or cooking pot
- mold - a picture frame with screen stapled over it or embroidery hoop or bent wire clothes hanger covered with an old stocking, and deckle – another frame on top
- pan or tub bigger than the mold
- couching materials – absorb water using newspapers covered with felt, dish towels, or other absorbent cloth
- rolling pin, smooth round stick, or board

Step 2: Gather –
- good wastepaper (envelopes, Christmas cards, scrap paper)
- dryer lint (if available)

Other suggestions to add -
- plant fibers (like seaweed, corn husks, cotton, rags, kudzu)
- animal fibers (like wool, horse hair, feathers, and dog hair)
- colorful yarn or string, glitter, dried flowers, etc.

Step 3: Tear or cut the wastepaper into small pieces. Fill the blender jar about 3/4 full of warm water. Add a big handful of the pieces of paper, a little handful of dryer lint, and some of the other fibers, if desired. Blend until pulp is smooth and fibers separated. For color add colored paper or fabric and blend for a few seconds.

If a blender is not available, the wastepaper and other plant fibers may be slowly cooked in a pot of water, about an hour, until the fibers turn to mush. Or the soaked paper and fibers may be beaten with a heavy stick until fibers separate. Mix in colors.

Experiment with different methods and materials. Record your data so that you can repeat the trials.

Step 4: You now have made *slurry*, a watery mixture of fibers. Pour this into the tub and then fill the tub with warm water. Mix the slurry and water until the fibers spread evenly. Slide the mold down into the tub and move it back and forth to get an even layer of fibers on the screen. Lift the mold and let the water pour through. Then you can press the pulp gently with your hand to squeeze out more water.

Another method is to hold the mold over the tub and pour the slurry evenly over the screen. Drain it until most of the water stops dripping, and then press the pulp gently with your hands.

Pour any leftover slurry water *outside* on the ground. It will clog up drain pipes!

Step 5: *Couch* the paper by flipping the mold over on to the couch cloth covering the newspaper. Lift the mold, leaving the pulp. Pressed flowers or other items you gathered could be added now. Cover the pulp with another couch cloth. Squeeze out the water by gently rolling with the rolling pin or pressing with a board. Change the couch cloth to soak up more water.

Step 6: Dry the paper sheet still protected by the couch cloth. Here are several ways. Lay the paper on a board and place it in the sun. Put the paper between two flat surfaces and stack weights on top or slowly iron on both sides (don't burn it).

Step 7: When the paper is dry, stretch the couch cloth gently from both ends. This stretching will loosen the paper sheet from the cloth. Gently peel off the paper. You have handmade paper!

Dye Fabric

"Moreover thou shalt make the tabernacle with ten curtains of fine twined linen, and blue, and purple, and scarlet…" Exodus 26:1.

"And thou shalt make a covering for the tent of rams' skins dyed red…" Exodus 26:14.

From these Scriptures, we see that color was important to God in His meeting place with the Israelites. The sails of the ships had colors. Banners had colors. Different colors had special meanings. Royalty wore purple and blue garments. The dyes for coloring came from certain animals and plants, such as the Murex shellfish for purple and almond leaves for yellow.

Activity: Using natural materials dye a shirt, bandana, or flag.

Step 1: Choose a white cotton shirt or cut a piece of white cotton fabric (like an old sheet) for a bandana (about 24" x 24" or 60 cm x 60 cm) or flag (See "Wave Your Flag" page 90.)

Step 2: Prepare fabric before dying with a *fixative* to "set" or keep the dye. Make a fixative of 1 part "white" vinegar to 4 parts water. For berries use 1/4 cup (60 ml) salt to 4 cups (1 liter) water. Simmer (gently boil) the fabric in the fixative for an hour in an enamel, stainless steel, or glass pot. Do not use a metal spoon to stir the fabric in either the fixative or the dye.

Rinse the fabric thoroughly.

Step 3: Decide what color or colors you want or what natural materials you want to use. Here is how to prepare the dye bath.

Cook (simmer) to make the dye, 1 part plant to 2 parts water —

- *Flowers* – Simmer flowers in water for 15 minutes.
- *Berries* – Simmer berries in water for 45 minutes.
- *Barks or nut hulls* – Break into small pieces and simmer in water for an hour or more.
- *Stems, twigs, roots, vines, or lichens* – Cut up and soak in water overnight. The next day simmer in the same water for one hour.

- *Coffee, tea, vegetables such as beets, spinach, or onion skins* – Simmer in water until the color is dark.

No cooking —

- *Mud or clay* – Mix water into clay and soak fabric for a day.
- *Grass* – Rub the material hard in green grass.
- *Flowers and leaves* – On a non-absorbent surface place fresh flowers and leaves in a pleasing arrangement of colors and shapes. Place fabric on top. Gently pound the fabric with a rubber mallet or flat board or stick until the color from the flowers and leaves comes through.
- *Berries or fruit juices* - Rub or squeeze the material in mashed berries or fruit juice.

Step 4: Wet the fabric first if the dye is in water. Dye the fabric according to a method in Step 3. The longer the fabric is in the dye the darker the color. Rubber gloves will keep your hands from being dyed also.

Step 5: Rinse fabric until the water runs clear. (If using the cooked method, cool the fabric in its cooking water first.)

Step 6: Wash fabric in cold water with gentle soap. Thoroughly rinse. Dry the fabric away from sunlight. Always wash and dry your dyed fabric this way. Ironing will help set the dye.

Step 7: Enjoy wearing your shirt or bandana or flying your flag.

Additional activities: Experiment with other plant materials for dyes, and other fabrics or yarns or reeds, such as cattails. Keep a record as in the chart below. A good scientist or craftsman should be able to repeat the experiment from his or her notes.

Dyeing Experience				
Dye material	Amount	Fabric	Procedure	Results

Sandals

"...put off thy shoes from off thy feet, for the place whereon thou standest is holy ground" Exodus 3:5.

"John answered, saying unto them all, I indeed baptize you with water; but one mightier than I cometh, the latchet [strap] of whose shoes I am not worthy to unloose..." Luke 3:16.

"And the angel said unto him [Peter]...bind on thy sandals..." Acts 12:8.

Shoes were not worn indoors in Bible times. When you entered a wealthy man's house, your sandals were removed and your feet were washed by a slave. A long journey wore out a pair of sandals on the rocky roads. A broken strap was likely to happen.

Activity: Make a pair of sandals to wear.

Step 1: Gather materials. What materials are available and simple to work with? What materials would last the longest?
Soles - leather, cork, bark, cardboard, or wood.
Straps - leather strips, cord, or heavy material strips.
Scissors or other cutting tool as needed for the material used.
Glue, stapler, awl, punch, or needle and lacing material.

Step 2: Decide on the style of sandal you want. Here are some suggestions of sandals used in Bible times.

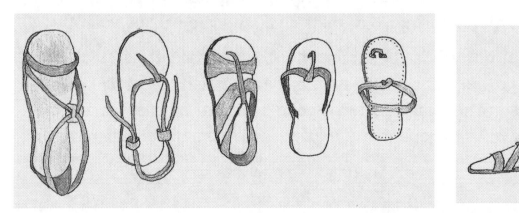
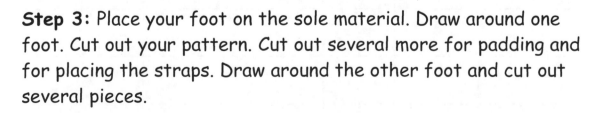

Step 3: Place your foot on the sole material. Draw around one foot. Cut out your pattern. Cut out several more for padding and for placing the straps. Draw around the other foot and cut out several pieces.

Step 4: For straps, measure your feet where straps will be placed, such as over the top of your foot, around heel, and/or over your big toe. Cut your strap material according to your pattern and your foot measurements, adding extra length for attaching to the sole on both sides.

Step 5: According to the pattern you are using, glue, staple, sew or lace the straps, between the sets of soles. Use an awl or punch if lacing through the soles.

Step 6: Glue or sew each set of soles together. Try on both sandals to check for fit. Make needed adjustments.

Step 7: Draw one of your sandals to show its style. What materials did you use? _____.

Step 8: Wear your handmade sandals for a while and make observations. Are they comfortable? _____.
Are they wearing out quickly? _____. Why? _____.
    What changes would you make next time and why?

"My Notes"

(Experiments, ideas, drawings, etc.)

111

What Next?

Index of Scriptures

Plan of Salvation

Index of Words

Map of Israel

Cut-Out Page

APPENDIX

What Next?

As you work through this book or have completed it, what can you to do next? Here are some ideas for you to try.

Most importantly, read the Bible every day. You will draw closer to God and all He wants to teach and share with you.

- Find more science in the Bible. (Job has a lot of observations.) Make up your own activities, demonstrations, and experiments. Write them down so others could experience them too.

- Keep a journal, recording things you observe or experience.

- Write to grandparents, friends, and teachers about your experiences. Ask about their science experiences.

- Make friends with a scientist or other adult with a science interest or hobby.

- Write short stories, poems, or songs about some things you have learned. Share with others.

- Create a newspaper, magazine, or booklet for your writings, discoveries and observations. Put your writing in two columns on the page, as magazines do.

- Teach younger children about science.

- Act out a play about a Bible-science story, such as Noah preparing for the flood or the Israelites making bricks in Egypt.

- Start a Bible-science club. Invite family and friends to share experiences. Choose a name and logo. Post on the internet? Ask an adult to help out (driving, gathering needed items, offering suggestions). Use the author's books as resources.

- Have a Bible-science party. The theme could be an activity or project in this book. Serve refreshments.

- Share this book with adults at church, Christian school, Bible camp, home-school group, or a missionary. See Contacts (page 127) to order more copies.

- Find places in your area to visit, like a museum, laboratory, visitor's center, farm, park, camp, _____.

- Start collections – science books and equipment, shells, seeds, pressed leaves and flowers, plants for dye colors, tree-shape drawings, rocks, and/or _____.

- Sleep outside (camp out), even in your back yard, and observe the night sounds, stars, temperature change, and moisture change. Did insects or other animals disturb your sleep?

- Draw pictures and/or take photographs. Capture different lighting, such as sunrise or sunset or shadows. Try unusual angles, like a snake's view. A picture can tell a story.

- Take photographs of clouds – types, colors, and fluffy shapes.

- Observe the weather – measure rainfall, check temperature, wind speed and direction, cloud cover, look at weather maps, make your forecast, and keep a daily record of the weather.

- You can write to the author with your comments, discoveries, suggestions, and orders. Visit the website for updates. Contact information is on page 127.

- What next? My notes:

Index of Scriptures

Color the hearts

Plan of Salvation

God has prepared a wonderful place for you to live in forever. It is heaven with streets of pure gold. (John 14:2, Revelation 21:21)

But you have sinned (told a lie, stole something, disobeyed your parents) so He cannot let you in. (Romans 3:23)

Jesus, God's Son, came to earth to die for your sins. His blood was shed on a cross for you. (Romans 5:8, 1 John 1:7)

If you pray to Jesus to come into your heart He will forgive you of all your sins. You will become clean. (Psalm 51:7)

Pray: "Jesus, I know I have sinned. I'm sorry and I want to change. I believe that You died for me on the cross and rose again from the grave. Please come into my heart and take over my life. I want to live with You forever in Heaven."

Now you can grow in knowing about Him. Read your Bible every day. Go to a church that teaches about God and Jesus. Pray to God and listen to what He tells you. (2 Peter 3:18)

116

Index of Words

118

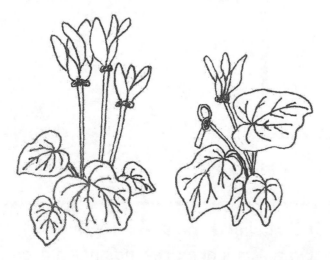

Wild pink
Cyclamens in
Israel

Map of Israel

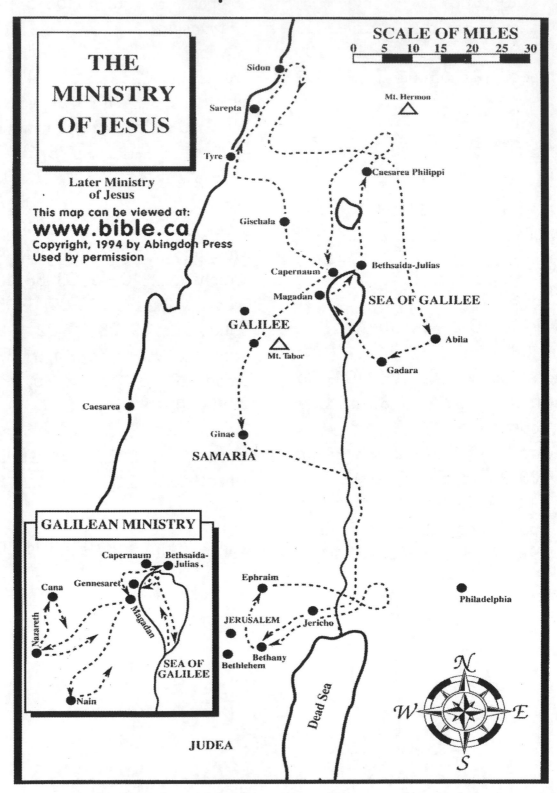

Look at this map of Israel and the satellite photo of the same area on the back cover. Maps are drawings of an area from above.

Cut-Out Page

Paste the items on cardboard (like a cereal box) for easier use.

Patch

Wear on your lab coat

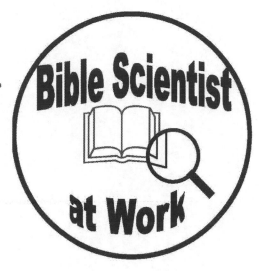

Protractor

Use inside numbers

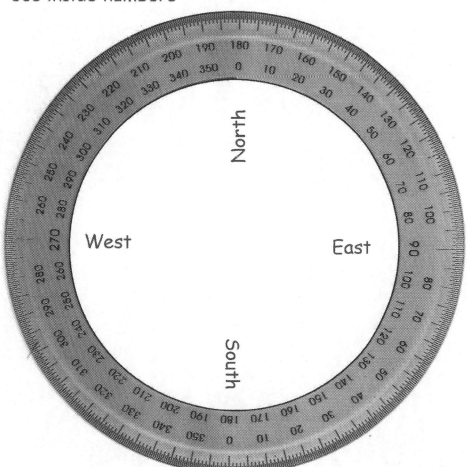

Ruler

126

Page left blank for gluing Cut-Out Page

Contacts

Books available by author:

Ages 6 to 10

All ages

Website: www.kidsbiblescience.com

Order books from:
Townsend Gift Shop
JAARS, Inc.
P.O. Box 248
Waxhaw, NC 28173

Phone: 704-843-6104

FAX: 704-843-6400
Att. Gift Shop

Or search online for bookstores:
"Experiencing Bible Science"

Contact author:
Mrs. Louise B. Derr
EBS Media, LLC
8808 Crossbow Lane
Waxhaw, NC 28173

Email:
EBS_Media@windstream.net